AIR
FRYER

AMAZING RECIPES
WITHOUT EXCESS FAT!

Publications International, Ltd.

Let's get social!

@Publications_International

@PublicationsInternational

www.pilcookbooks.com

Contents

Enjoy your air fryer

Do you love fried foods but try to avoid them? You no longer need to worry.

The air fryer is your answer to preparing fried foods without the extra calories, fat, or mess in the kitchen. You'll get the taste, and texture of fried foods—crispy, tasty, and crunchy—that you love and crave, without the added guilt often felt when consuming them. Plus, you'll soon see how your air fryer is so easy to use, cooks food faster, and provides a no-fuss clean up.

You'll love the ability to prepare fried foods in your air fryer, but you'll also soon find that you can prepare all types of other foods, too. Make everything from appetizers to meals to sides and even desserts! Why not try cookies or muffins? What about trying marinated salmon or a tuna melt? You'll even love the taste of roasted vegetables. You can bake in it, grill in it, steam in it, roast in it, and reheat in it.

Choose from more than 100 ideas here, or create your own.

Now get started and have fun eating and serving all those healthier foods without the added guilt.

Helpful Tips:

- Read your air fryer's manufacturer's directions carefully before cooking to make sure you understand the specific features of your air fryer before starting to cook.

- Preheat your air fryer for 2 to 3 minutes before cooking.

- You can cook foods typically cooked in the oven in your air fryer. But because the air fryer is more condensed than a regular oven, it is recommended that recipes cut 25°F to 50°F off temperature and 20% off the typical cooking times.

- Avoid having foods stick to your air fryer basket by using nonstick cooking spray or cooking on parchment paper or foil. You can also get food to brown and crisp more easily by spraying occasionally with nonstick cooking spray during the cooking process.

- Don't overfill your basket. Each air fryer differs in its basket size. Cook foods in batches as needed.

- Use toothpicks to hold food in place. You may notice that light foods may blow around from the pressure of the fan. Just be sure to secure foods in the basket to prevent this.

- Check foods while cooking by opening the air fryer basket. This will not disturb cooking times. Once you return the basket, the cooking resumes.

- Experiment with cooking times of various foods. Test foods for doneness before consuming—check meats and poultry with a meat thermometer, and use a toothpick to test muffins and cupcakes.

- Use your air fryer to cook frozen foods, too! Frozen French fries, fish sticks, chicken nuggets, individual pizzas—these all work great. Just remember to reduce cooking temperatures and times.

Estimated Cooking Temperatures/Times*

Food	Temperature	Timing
Vegetables (asparagus, broccoli, corn-on-cob, green beans, mushrooms, cherry tomatoes)	390°F	5 to 6 min.
Vegetables (bell peppers, cauliflower, eggplant, onions, potatoes, zucchini)	390°F	8 to 12 min.
Chicken (bone-in)	370°F	20 to 25 min.
Chicken (boneless)	370°F	12 to 15 min.
Beef (ground beef)	370°F	15 to 17 min.
Beef (steaks, roasts)	390°F	10 to 15 min.
Pork	370°F	12 to 15 min.
Fish	390°F	10 to 12 min.
Frozen Foods	390°F	10 to 15 min.

*This is just a guide. All food varies in size, weight, and texture. Be sure to test your food for preferred doneness before consuming it. Also, some foods will need to be shaken or flipped to help distribute ingredients for proper cooking.

Make note of the temperatures and times that work best for you for continued success of your air fryer.

Enjoy and have fun!

Mozzarella Sticks

MAKES 4 TO 6 SERVINGS

¼	cup all-purpose flour	½	teaspoon salt
2	eggs	½	teaspoon garlic powder
1	tablespoon water	1	package (12 ounces) string cheese (12 sticks)
1	cup plain dry bread crumbs		
2	teaspoons Italian seasoning	1	cup marinara or pizza sauce, heated

1. Place flour in shallow dish. Whisk eggs and water in another shallow dish. Combine bread crumbs, Italian seasoning, salt and garlic powder in third shallow dish.

2. Coat each piece of cheese with flour. Dip in egg mixture, letting excess drip back into bowl. Roll in bread crumb mixture to coat. Dip again in egg mixture and roll again in bread crumb mixture. Refrigerate until ready to cook.

3. Preheat air fryer to 370°F. Line basket with parchment paper; spray with nonstick cooking spray.

4. Cook in batches 8 to 10 minutes, shaking halfway through cooking, until golden brown. Serve with marinara sauce.

Caprese-Style Tartlets

MAKES 6 TARTLETS

3 tomatoes, cut into 4 slices each

3 tablespoons prepared pesto sauce

1 sheet frozen puff pastry (half of 17¼-ounce package)

6 ounces fresh mozzarella cheese

2 tablespoons chopped kalamata olives

1. Place tomatoes in large resealable food storage bag. Add pesto; toss to coat. Marinate at room temperature 30 minutes.

2. Unfold puff pastry; thaw 20 minutes on lightly floured surface.

3. Preheat air fryer to 370°F. Line basket with parchment paper.

4. Cut out six 4-inch rounds from pastry. Top each round with two tomato slices. Cook in batches 8 to 10 minutes or until pastry is light golden and puffed.

5. Cut cheese into six ¼-inch-thick slices. Top each tart with one cheese slice. Cook in batches 1 minute or until cheese is melted. Top tarts evenly with olives. Serve warm.

Citrus Candied Nuts

MAKES ABOUT 3 CUPS

1 egg white	2 tablespoons lemon juice
1½ cups whole almonds	2 teaspoons grated orange peel
1½ cups pecan halves	1 teaspoon grated lemon peel
1 cup powdered sugar	⅛ teaspoon ground nutmeg

1. Beat egg white in medium bowl with electric mixer at high speed until soft peaks form. Add almonds and pecans; stir until well coated. Stir in powdered sugar, lemon juice, orange peel, lemon peel and nutmeg until evenly coated.

2. Preheat air fryer to 350°F. Spray basket with nonstick cooking spray.

3. Cook 6 to 8 minutes, stirring and shaking several times during cooking, until nuts are lightly browned. Remove nuts to bowl or tray to cool. Cool completely. Store in airtight container up to 2 weeks.

The Big Onion
MAKES 6 SERVINGS

Dipping Sauce
- ½ cup light mayonnaise
- 2 tablespoons horseradish
- 1 tablespoon ketchup
- ¼ teaspoon paprika
- ⅛ teaspoon salt
- ⅛ teaspoon ground red pepper
- ⅛ teaspoon dried oregano

Onion
- 1 large sweet onion (about 1 pound)
- ½ cup all-purpose flour
- 1 tablespoon buttermilk
- 2 eggs
- ½ cup panko bread crumbs
- 1 tablespoon paprika
- 1½ teaspoons seafood seasoning

1. For sauce, combine mayonnaise, horseradish, ketchup, ¼ teaspoon paprika, salt, ground red pepper and oregano in small bowl; mix well. Cover and refrigerate until ready to serve.

2. For onion, cut about ½ inch off top of onion and peel off papery skin. Place onion cut side down on cutting board. Starting ½ inch from root, use large sharp knife to make one slice down to cutting board. Repeat slicing all the way around onion to make 12 to 16 evenly spaced cuts. Turn onion over; gently separate outer pieces.

3. Meanwhile, put flour in large bowl. Whisk buttermilk and eggs in another large bowl. Combine panko, 1 tablespoon paprika and seafood seasoning in another bowl.

4. Coat onion with flour, shaking off any excess. Dip entire onion in egg mixture, letting excess drip back into bowl. Then, coat evenly with panko.

5. Preheat air fryer to 390°F. Spray basket with nonstick cooking spray.

6. Cook 10 to 12 minutes or until golden brown and crispy. Serve immediately with dipping sauce.

Garlic Bites

MAKES 24 TO 27 APPETIZERS

½ of 16-ounce package frozen phyllo dough, thawed to room temperature

¾ cup (1½ sticks) butter, melted

3 large heads garlic, separated into cloves, peeled

½ cup finely chopped walnuts

1 cup Italian-style bread crumbs

1. Remove phyllo from package; unroll and place on large sheet of waxed paper. Cut phyllo crosswise into 2-inch-wide strips. Cover phyllo with large sheet of plastic wrap and damp, clean kitchen towel. (Phyllo dries out quickly if not covered.)

2. Lay 1 strip of phyllo at a time on flat surface and brush immediately with butter. Place 1 clove of garlic at end. Sprinkle 1 teaspoon walnuts along length of strip.

3. Roll up garlic clove and walnuts in strip, tucking in side edges as you roll. Brush with butter; roll in bread crumbs. Repeat with remaining phyllo, garlic, walnuts, butter and bread crumbs.

4. Preheat air fryer to 350°F. Cook in batches 6 to 8 minutes or until golden brown. Cool slightly.

Lavash Chips with Artichoke Pesto

MAKES 6 SERVINGS (ABOUT 1½ CUPS PESTO)

3 pieces lavash bread

¼ cup plus 2 tablespoons olive oil, divided

¾ teaspoon kosher salt, divided

1 can (14 ounces) artichoke hearts, rinsed and drained

½ cup chopped walnuts, toasted*

¼ cup packed fresh basil leaves

1 clove garlic, minced

2 tablespoons lemon juice

¼ cup grated Parmesan cheese

To toast nuts, cook in preheated 350°F parchment-lined air fryer 3 to 4 minutes until golden brown.

1. Preheat air fryer to 370°F. Line basket with parchment paper.

2. Brush both sides of lavash with 2 tablespoons oil. Sprinkle with ¼ teaspoon salt. Cut to fit in air fryer, if necessary. Cook in batches 8 to 10 minutes, shaking occasionally, until lavash is crisp and browned. Cool on wire rack.

3. Place artichoke hearts, walnuts, basil, garlic, lemon juice and remaining ½ teaspoon salt in food processor; pulse about 12 times until coarsely chopped. While food processor is running, slowly stream remaining ¼ cup oil until smooth. Add cheese and pulse until blended.

4. Serve lavash with pesto.

Note: You can also toast walnuts in preheated 350°F oven 6 to 8 minutes, if preferred.

Garlic-Herb Parmesan Dipping Sticks

MAKES 12 SERVINGS

1 package (about 14 ounces) refrigerated pizza dough

All-purpose flour, for dusting

¾ cup light garlic-and-herb spreadable cheese

¾ cup (3 ounces) shredded Italian cheese blend

¼ cup grated Parmesan cheese

½ teaspoon dried oregano

Warm marinara sauce and/ or ranch salad dressing (optional)

1. Roll out dough on lightly floured surface to 12-inch square. Spread garlic-and-herb spreadable cheese evenly over bread. Top with Italian cheese blend, Parmesan cheese and oregano.

2. Preheat air fryer to 390°F. Line basket with parchment paper; spray with nonstick cooking spray.

3. Cut dough in half or thirds to fit into basket. Cook in batches 6 to 8 minutes or until golden brown. Let cool slightly.

4. Slice lengthwise into strips. Serve with marinara sauce or ranch for dipping, if desired.

Meatball Mummies

MAKES ABOUT 20 MUMMIES

1 can (15 ounces) refrigerated crescent roll dough

1 package (20 ounces) frozen meatballs

Black olive slices

1 tablespoon marinara sauce, plus additional for dipping

1. Unroll dough onto large cutting board. Press seams together; cut lengthwise into 20 strips. Wrap each meatball with one strip of dough, stretching dough to circle meatballs.

2. Dip olives into 1 tablespoon of marinara sauce. Place 2 olive slices on each meatball for eyes.

3. Preheat air fryer to 370°F. Line basket with parchment paper.

4. Cook in batches 8 to 10 minutes or until golden brown. Serve with additional marinara sauce.

Sausage Rolls

MAKES 4 SERVINGS

8 ounces ground pork

¼ cup finely chopped onion

½ teaspoon coarse salt

1 teaspoon minced garlic

½ teaspoon dried thyme

½ teaspoon dried basil

¼ teaspoon dried marjoram

¼ teaspoon black pepper

1 sheet frozen puff pastry (half of 17¼-ounce package), thawed

1 egg, beaten

1. Combine pork, onion, salt, garlic, thyme, basil, marjoram and pepper in medium bowl; mix well.

2. Place puff pastry on floured surface; cut lengthwise into three strips at seams. Roll each third into 10×4½-inch rectangle. Shape one third of pork mixture into 10-inch log; arrange log along top edge of one pastry rectangle. Brush bottom ½ inch of rectangle with egg. Roll pastry down around pork; press to seal. Cut each roll crosswise into four pieces. Repeat with remaining puff pastry and pork mixture. Brush top of each roll with egg.

3. Preheat air fryer to 370°F. Line basket with parchment paper.

4. Cook in batches 8 to 10 minutes or until sausage is cooked through and pastry is golden brown and puffed. Remove to wire rack; cool 10 minutes. Serve warm.

Bacon-Wrapped Teriyaki Shrimp

MAKES 6 SERVINGS

1 pound large raw shrimp,
  peeled and deveined
  (with tails on)

¼ cup teriyaki marinade

12 slices bacon, cut in half
  crosswise

1. Place shrimp in large resealable food storage bag. Add teriyaki marinade; seal bag and turn to coat. Marinate in refrigerator 15 to 20 minutes.

2. Remove shrimp from bag; reserve marinade. Wrap each shrimp with one piece bacon. Brush bacon with some of reserved marinade.

3. Preheat air fryer to 390°F. Line basket with parchment paper or foil; spray lightly with nonstick cooking spray.

4. Cook 4 to 6 minutes or until bacon is crisp and shrimp are pink and opaque.

Tip: Do not use thick-cut bacon for this recipe, because the bacon will not be completely cooked when the shrimp are cooked through.

Warm Goat Cheese Rounds

MAKES 4 SERVINGS

1 package (4 ounces) garlic herb goat cheese

1 egg

1 tablespoon water

⅓ cup seasoned dry bread crumbs

Marinara sauce

1. Cut cheese crosswise into eight slices. (If cheese is too difficult to slice, shape scant tablespoonfuls of cheese into balls and flatten into ¼-inch-thick rounds.)

2. Beat egg and water in small bowl. Place bread crumbs in shallow dish. Dip cheese rounds into egg mixture, then in bread crumbs, turning to coat all sides. Gently press bread crumbs to adhere. Place coated rounds on plate; freeze 10 minutes.

3. Preheat air fryer to 370°F. Cook in batches 10 minutes, flipping halfway through cooking, until golden brown. Serve immediately with marinara sauce.

Toasted Ravioli

MAKES 4 TO 5 SERVINGS

1 cup all-purpose flour

2 eggs

¼ cup water

1 cup plain dry bread crumbs

1 teaspoon Italian seasoning

¾ teaspoon garlic powder

¼ teaspoon salt

½ cup grated Parmesan cheese

2 tablespoons finely chopped fresh parsley (optional)

1 package (10 ounces) meat or cheese ravioli, thawed if frozen

Pasta sauce, heated

1. Place flour in shallow dish. Whisk eggs and water in another shallow dish. Combine bread crumbs, Italian seasoning, garlic powder and salt in third shallow dish. Combine Parmesan cheese and parsley, if desired, in large bowl.

2. Preheat air fryer to 390°F. Poke holes in ravioli with toothpick.

3. Coat ravioli with flour. Dip in egg mixture, letting excess drip back into bowl. Roll in bread crumb mixture to coat. Spray with nonstick cooking spray.

4. Cook in batches 5 to 6 minutes, turning once, until golden brown. Add to bowl with cheese; toss to coat. Serve warm with sauce.

Falafel Nuggets

MAKES 12 SERVINGS

Sauce

2½ cups tomato sauce
⅓ cup tomato paste
2 tablespoons lemon juice
2 teaspoons sugar
1 teaspoon onion powder
½ teaspoon salt

Falafel

2 cans (about 15 ounces each) chickpeas, rinsed and drained

½ cup all-purpose flour
½ cup chopped fresh parsley
1 egg
¼ cup minced onion
3 tablespoons lemon juice
2 tablespoons minced garlic
2 teaspoons ground cumin
½ teaspoon salt
½ teaspoon ground red pepper or red pepper flakes

1. For sauce, combine tomato sauce, tomato paste, 2 tablespoons lemon juice, sugar, onion powder and ½ teaspoon salt in medium saucepan. Simmer over medium-low heat 20 minutes or until heated through. Cover and keep warm until ready to serve.

2. For falafel, combine chickpeas, flour, parsley, egg, minced onion, 3 tablespoons lemon juice, garlic, cumin, ½ teaspoon salt and ground red pepper in food processor or blender; process until well blended. Shape mixture into 1-inch balls. Spray with nonstick cooking spray.

3. Preheat air fryer to 390°F. Line basket with foil; spray with cooking spray.

4. Cook in batches 12 to 15 minutes, turning halfway through cooking, until browned. Serve with sauce.

Grilled Cheese Kabobs

MAKES 12 SERVINGS

8 thick slices whole wheat bread

3 thick slices sharp Cheddar cheese

3 thick slices Monterey Jack or Colby Jack cheese

2 tablespoons butter, melted

1. Cut each slice bread into 1-inch squares. Cut each slice cheese into 1-inch squares. Make small sandwiches with one square of bread and one square of each type of cheese. Top with second square of bread. Brush sandwiches with butter.

2. Preheat air fryer to 370°F. Cook sandwich squares 30 seconds to 1 minute until golden brown and cheese is slightly melted.

3. Place sandwiches on the ends of short wooden skewers, if desired, or eat as finger food.

Pepperoni Bread
MAKES ABOUT 6 SERVINGS

1 package (about 14 ounces) refrigerated pizza dough

All-purpose flour, for dusting

8 slices provolone cheese

20 to 30 slices pepperoni (about ½ of 6-ounce package)

¾ cup (3 ounces) shredded mozzarella cheese

½ cup grated Parmesan cheese

½ teaspoon Italian seasoning

1 egg, beaten

Marinara sauce, heated

1. Preheat air fryer to 390°F. Line basket with parchment paper. Unroll pizza dough on lightly floured surface; cut dough in half.

2. Working with one half at a time, arrange half the provolone slices on half the dough. Top with half the pepperoni, half the mozzarella and Parmesan cheeses and half the Italian seasoning. Repeat with other half bread and toppings.

3. Fold top half of dough over filling; press edges with fork or pinch edges to seal. Transfer one bread to basket. Brush with egg.

4. Cook 8 to 10 minutes or until crust is golden brown. Remove to wire rack to cool slightly. Repeat with other bread. Cut crosswise into slices; serve warm with marinara sauce.

Mini Egg Rolls
MAKES 28 MINI EGG ROLLS

½ pound ground pork
3 cloves garlic, minced
1 teaspoon minced fresh ginger
¼ teaspoon red pepper flakes
6 cups (12 ounces) shredded coleslaw mix
¼ cup reduced-sodium soy sauce

1 tablespoon cornstarch
1 tablespoon seasoned rice vinegar
½ cup chopped green onions
28 wonton wrappers
Prepared sweet and sour sauce
Chinese hot mustard

1. Combine pork, garlic, ginger and red pepper flakes in large nonstick skillet; cook and stir over medium heat about 4 minutes or until pork is cooked through, stirring to break up meat. Add coleslaw mix; cover and cook 2 minutes. Uncover and cook 2 minutes or until coleslaw mix just begins to wilt.

2. Whisk soy sauce and cornstarch in small bowl until smooth and well blended; stir into pork mixture. Add vinegar; cook 2 to 3 minutes or until sauce is thickened. Remove from heat; stir in green onions.

3. Working with one wonton wrapper at a time, place wrapper on clean work surface. Spoon 1 level tablespoon pork mixture across and just below center of wrapper. Fold bottom point of wrapper up over filling; fold side points over filling, forming envelope shape. Moisten inside edges of top point with water and roll egg roll toward top point, pressing firmly to seal. Repeat with remaining wrappers and filling. Spray egg rolls with nonstick cooking spray.

4. Preheat air fryer to 370°F. Cook in batches 3 to 5 minutes until golden brown. Remove to cooling rack; cool slightly before serving. Serve with sweet and sour sauce and mustard for dipping.

Baked Salami

MAKES 5 SERVINGS

1 all-beef kosher salami (14 to 16 ounces)

½ cup apricot preserves

1 tablespoon hot pepper sauce

2 tablespoons packed brown sugar

Bread slices

1. Preheat air fryer to 370°F. Peel off plastic wrap of salami. Cut 12 crosswise (½-inch-deep) slits across top. Place, cut side up, in small dish that fits inside air fryer.

2. Combine preserves, hot pepper sauce and brown sugar in small bowl; stir well. Spoon sauce over top.

3. Cook 8 to 10 minutes or until juicy and dark brown, spooning sauce over salami occasionally during cooking.

4. Cut salami into thin slices; toss with sauce. Serve on bread.

Extras: Serve with slices of challah bread or cocktail rye.

Piggies in a Basket
MAKES 4 SERVINGS

1 can (8 ounces) refrigerated crescent rolls

1 package (about 12 ounces) cocktail franks

1. Preheat air fryer to 350°F.

2. Cut crescent dough into strips. Wrap dough around each frank.

3. Cook in batches 3 to 4 minutes or until golden brown.

Baked Orange Brie Appetizer

MAKES 6 SERVINGS

1 sheet puff pastry (half of 17¼-ounce package), thawed

⅓ cup orange marmalade

2 tablespoons chopped pecans (optional)

1 round (8 ounces) Brie cheese

1 egg white, beaten

1. Roll out puff pastry to 12-inch square. Use knife to cut off four corners; set aside scraps.

2. Spread marmalade over center of pastry to 1 inch of edges. Sprinkle pecans over marmalade, if desired. Place Brie in center on top of pecans. Brush exposed dough with egg white.

3. Gather up edges of puff pastry and bring together over center of Brie, covering cheese entirely. Pinch and twist pastry edges together to seal. Use dough scraps to decorate top of Brie. Brush lightly with egg white.

4. Preheat air fryer to 370°F.

5. Cook 8 to 10 minutes or until golden brown. Serve warm.

Biscuit Doughnuts

MAKES 8 DOUGHNUTS

---

1 package (about 16 ounces) refrigerated jumbo biscuit dough (8 biscuits)

¼ cup honey

1 teaspoon chopped pistachio nuts

---

1. Separate dough into eight portions. Using hands, create a hole in the middle to create doughnut shape.

2. Preheat air fryer to 370°F.

3. Cook in batches 7 to 8 minutes or until golden brown.

4. Drizzle warm doughnuts with honey. Sprinkle with pistachios.

Variation: For cinnamon-sugar coating, combine ¼ cup sugar and 1 teaspoon ground cinnamon in small bowl. Dip warm doughnuts in cinnamon-sugar topping while warm.

Raspberry Puffs

MAKES 8 PUFFS

1 package (8 ounces) refrigerated crescent roll dough

¼ cup raspberry fruit spread

½ of an 8-ounce package cream cheese, softened

1 to 2 teaspoons sugar

2 tablespoons reduced-fat (2%) milk

¼ teaspoon vanilla

1. Separate crescent roll dough into eight triangles; unroll on lightly floured surface. Brush 1½ teaspoons fruit spread evenly over each roll. Roll up each triangle, starting at wide end.

2. Preheat air fryer to 370°F. Line basket with parchment paper.

3. Cook in batches 5 to 6 minutes or until lightly golden. Cool.

4. Meanwhile, whisk together cream cheese, sugar, milk and vanilla in small bowl until smooth. Spoon about 1 tablespoon cream cheese mixture over each cooled roll or serve on the side, as desired.

Variation: For an even lighter-tasting roll, replace the cream cheese mixture with powdered sugar. Simply sprinkle 2 tablespoons evenly over all.

Apple Butter Rolls

MAKES 12 SERVINGS

1 package (about 11 ounces) refrigerated breadstick dough (12 breadsticks)

2 tablespoons apple butter

¼ cup sifted powdered sugar

1 to 1½ teaspoons orange juice

¼ teaspoon grated orange peel (optional)

1. Unroll breadstick dough; separate into 12 pieces along perforations. Gently stretch each piece to 9 inches in length. Twist ends of each piece in opposite directions three or four times. Coil each twisted strip into snail shape; tuck ends underneath. Use thumb to make small indentation in center of each breadstick coil. Spoon about ½ teaspoon apple butter into each indentation.

2. Preheat air fryer to 370°F. Line basket with parchment paper; spray with nonstick cooking spray.

3. Cook in batches 8 to 10 minutes or until golden brown. Remove to wire rack; cool 10 minutes.

4. Meanwhile, combine powdered sugar and 1 teaspoon orange juice in small bowl; whisk until smooth. Add additional orange juice, if necessary, to make pourable glaze. Stir in orange peel, if desired. Drizzle glaze over rolls. Serve warm.

Easy Raspberry-Peach Danish

MAKES 8 SERVINGS

1 package (8 ounces) refrigerated crescent dough sheet

¼ cup raspberry fruit spread

1 can (about 15 ounces) sliced peaches in juice, drained and chopped

1 egg white, beaten

½ cup powdered sugar

2 to 3 teaspoons orange juice

¼ cup chopped pecans, toasted*

To toast nuts, cook in preheated 350°F parchment-lined air fryer 3 to 4 minutes until golden brown.

1. Place dough on lightly floured surface; cut in half. Roll each half into 12×8-inch rectangle.

2. Spread half of raspberry spread over center third of each dough rectangle; top with peaches. Make 2-inch-long cuts from edges towards filling on long sides of each dough rectangle at 1-inch intervals. Fold strips of dough over filling. Brush with egg white.

3. Preheat air fryer to 370°F. Line basket with parchment paper. Cook in batches 5 to 7 minutes or until golden brown. Remove to wire rack; cool slightly.

4. Combine powdered sugar and enough orange juice in small bowl to make pourable glaze. Drizzle glaze over Danish; sprinkle with pecans.

Quick Chocolate Chip Sticky Buns

MAKES ABOUT 12 STICKY BUNS

1 package (about 11 ounces) refrigerated French bread dough

¼ cup sugar

1 teaspoon ground cinnamon

½ cup mini semisweet chocolate chips

2 tablespoons butter

⅓ cup chopped pecans, toasted*

1 tablespoon maple syrup

*To toast nuts, cook in preheated 350°F parchment-lined air fryer 3 to 4 minutes until golden brown.

1. Unroll dough on lightly floured large cutting board or clean work surface. Combine sugar and cinnamon in small bowl; sprinkle evenly over dough. Top with chocolate chips. Starting with short side, roll up dough jelly-roll style. Cut crosswise into 12 (¾-inch) slices with serrated knife.

2. Combine butter, pecans and maple syrup in small bowl; mix well.

3. Preheat air fryer to 370°F. Line basket with parchment paper; spray with nonstick cooking spray.

4. Arrange dough slices cut sides up in basket, brush butter mixture over top of rolls. Cook 8 to 10 minutes or until golden brown. Serve warm.

Raspberry White Chocolate Danish

MAKES 8 SERVINGS

1 package (8 ounces) refrigerated crescent roll dough

8 teaspoons red raspberry preserves

1 ounce white baking chocolate, chopped

1. Unroll crescent dough; separate into eight triangles. Place 1 teaspoon preserves in center of each triangle. Fold right and left corners of long side over filling to top corner to form rectangle. Pinch edges to seal.

2. Preheat air fryer to 370°F. Line basket with parchment paper; spray with nonstick cooking spray.

3. Cook, seam side up, in batches 5 to 7 minutes or until lightly browned. Remove to wire rack to cool 5 minutes.

4. Place white chocolate in small resealable food storage bag. Microwave on MEDIUM (50%) 1 minute; gently knead bag. Microwave and knead at additional 30-second intervals until chocolate is completely melted. Cut off small corner of bag; drizzle chocolate over danish.

Strawberry Cheese Danishes

MAKES 8 SERVINGS

½ cup cream cheese, softened
2 tablespoons granulated sugar
2 teaspoons lemon juice
½ teaspoon grated lemon peel

1 package (8 ounces) refrigerated crescent roll dough
8 teaspoons strawberry preserves
Powdered sugar (optional)

1. Combine cream cheese, granulated sugar, lemon juice and lemon peel in small bowl.

2. Separate dough into four rectangles; press perforations to seal. Working with one piece of dough at a time, spread each rectangle with 2 tablespoons cream cheese mixture. Roll up lengthwise, pinching edge and ends to seal. Carefully stretch each roll to about 12 inches. Cut each in half.

3. Shape halves into spirals, tucking ends under. Make indentation in center of each roll; fill with 1 teaspoon preserves.

4. Preheat air fryer to 370°F. Cook in batches 5 to 7 minutes or until lightly browned. Remove to wire rack. Cool slightly. Sprinkle rolls with powdered sugar, if desired.

Variation: Any flavor preserves may be used in place of the strawberry preserves.

Apple-Cranberry Turnovers

MAKES 4 TURNOVERS

1 sheet puff pastry (half of 17¼-ounce package), thawed

Filling

1 large Granny Smith apple (about 7 ounces), peeled and diced (about 1 cup)

2 tablespoons dried cranberries

2 tablespoons packed dark brown sugar

1 tablespoon butter

¼ teaspoon ground cinnamon

⅛ teaspoon ground allspice

Topping

1½ teaspoons granulated sugar

⅛ teaspoon ground cinnamon

1 tablespoon butter, melted

1. Unfold puff pastry.

2. Place filling ingredients in medium saucepan. Cook and stir 2 to 3 minutes over medium heat until apples start to soften. Remove from heat; cool completely.

3. Cut dough into four squares. Brush edges with water. Spoon ¼ cup of the apple mixture in center of each square and fold dough to create a triangle. Seal edges by pinching seams with fork. Place on baking sheet. Cover and refrigerate 30 minutes.

4. Preheat air fryer to 370°F. Remove turnovers from refrigerator. Make small cut on top of each turnover. Cook in batches 8 to 10 minutes or until puffed and golden brown.

5. For topping, combine granulated sugar and cinnamon in small bowl. Brush equal amounts of butter on each warm turnover; sprinkle with cinnamon-sugar mixture. Serve warm or at room temperature.

Cinnamini Buns

MAKES 2 DOZEN

2 tablespoons packed brown sugar

½ teaspoon ground cinnamon

1 package (8 ounces) refrigerated crescent roll dough

1 tablespoon butter, melted

½ cup powdered sugar

1 to 1½ tablespoons milk

1. Combine brown sugar and cinnamon in small bowl; mix well.

2. Unroll dough and separate into two 12×4-inch rectangles; firmly press perforations to seal. Brush dough with butter; sprinkle with brown sugar mixture. Starting with long side, roll up tightly jelly-roll style; pinch seams to seal. Cut each roll crosswise into 12 (1-inch) slices with serrated knife.

3. Preheat air fryer to 370°F. Line basket with parchment paper.

4. Cook, seam side up, in batches 5 to 7 minutes or until golden brown. Remove to wire rack; cool.

5. Combine powdered sugar and 1 tablespoon milk in small bowl; whisk until smooth. Add additional milk, 1 teaspoon at a time, to reach desired glaze consistency. Drizzle glaze over buns.

Quick Jelly-Filled Biscuit Doughnut Balls

MAKES 20 DOUGHNUT BALLS

1 package (about 7 ounces) refrigerated reduced-fat biscuit dough (10 biscuits)

¼ cup coarse sugar

1 cup strawberry preserves*

*If preserves are very chunky, process in food processor 10 seconds or press through fine-mesh sieve.

1. Preheat air fryer to 370°F.

2. Separate biscuits into ten portions. Cut each in half; roll dough into balls to create 20 balls.

3. Cook in batches 5 to 6 minutes or until golden brown.

4. Place sugar in large bowl. Coat warm balls in sugar. Let cool. Using a piping bag with medium star tip; fill bag with preserves. Poke hole in side of each doughnut ball with paring knife; fill with preserves. Serve immediately.

Breakfast Flats

MAKES 4 SERVINGS

1 package (about 14 ounces) refrigerated pizza dough

All-purpose flour, for dusting

1½ cups (6 ounces) shredded medium Cheddar cheese

8 slices bacon, cooked crisp and diced (optional)

4 eggs, fried

Kosher salt and black pepper (optional)

1. Divide pizza dough into four equal portions. Roll out on lightly floured surface into rectangles roughly 8½×4 inches. Top each evenly with cheese and bacon, if desired.

2. Preheat air fryer to 370°F. Line basket with parchment paper.

3. Cook in batches 5 to 7 minutes or until crust is golden brown and crisp and cheese is melted.

4. Top baked flats with fried egg; season with salt and pepper, if desired. Serve warm.

Crunchy French Toast Sticks

MAKES 6 SERVINGS

6 slices Italian bread (each 1 inch thick, about 3½ to 4 inches in diameter)

4 cups cornflakes, crushed

3 eggs

⅔ cup reduced-fat (2%) milk

1 tablespoon sugar

1 teaspoon vanilla

1 teaspoon ground cinnamon, plus additional for serving

¼ teaspoon ground nutmeg

1 container (6 ounces) vanilla yogurt

¼ cup maple syrup

1. Remove crusts from bread, if desired. Cut each bread slice into three strips. Place cornflakes on waxed paper.

2. Whisk eggs, milk, sugar, vanilla, 1 teaspoon cinnamon and nutmeg in shallow dish. Dip bread strips in egg mixture, turning to generously coat all sides. Roll in cornflakes, coating all sides.

3. Preheat air fryer to 370°F. Cook in batches 8 to 10 minutes, turning halfway through cooking or until golden brown.

4. Meanwhile, combine yogurt and maple syrup in small bowl. Sprinkle with additional cinnamon, if desired. Serve French toast sticks with yogurt mixture.

Breakfast Burritos

MAKES 4 SERVINGS

4 **turkey breakfast sausage links**	4 **(6-inch) yellow or white corn tortillas**
2 **eggs**	¼ **cup salsa**
½ **teaspoon ground cumin (optional)**	

1. Preheat air fryer to 370°F. Line basket with parchment paper.

2. Cook sausages 6 to 8 minutes or until browned on the outside and cooked through, shaking occasionally during cooking. Remove sausages to plate.

3. Whisk eggs and cumin, if desired, in small bowl. Heat small skillet over medium-high heat. Cook eggs until done.

4. Place sausage link in middle of each tortilla. Spoon equal amounts of scrambled egg on top of sausage. Roll up to enclose the filling; secure with toothpick.

5. Cook in air fryer 2 to 3 minutes or until heated through.

6. Pour salsa in small bowl. Serve with burritos.

Sweet Breakfast Tacos: Substitute four 4-inch frozen pancakes for the tortillas and ¼ cup light maple syrup for the salsa. Prepare the sausages and the eggs as directed. Stack pancakes on microwaveable plate. Microwave on HIGH 30 to 60 seconds or until warmed through. To assemble tacos, place pancake on flat surface. Place sausage link in middle of pancake. Spoon 2 tablespoons egg along length of sausage. Fold in half. Repeat with remaining pancakes, sausages and egg. Pour maple syrup into small bowl. Serve on side for dipping or for drizzling over tacos.

Peanut Butter and Jelly French Toast
MAKES 6 SERVINGS

- 1 banana, sliced
- 2 tablespoons peanuts, chopped
- 2 tablespoons orange juice
- 1 tablespoon honey
- 6 slices whole wheat bread
- ¼ cup grape jelly (or favorite flavor)
- ¼ cup peanut butter
- 2 eggs
- ¼ cup milk

1. Combine banana, peanuts, orange juice and honey in small bowl; set aside. Spread 3 bread slices with jelly and 3 slices with peanut butter. Press peanut butter and jelly slices together to form 3 sandwiches; cut each sandwich in half diagonally.

2. Beat eggs and milk in shallow dish. Dip sandwiches in egg mixture, turning to coat.

3. Preheat air fryer to 350°F. Line basket with parchment paper.

4. Cook in batches 3 to 4 minutes per side or until light golden brown. Top with banana mixture.

Biscuit Breakfast Pizzas

MAKES 8 SERVINGS

1 package (about 16 ounces) refrigerated flaky biscuit dough

8 tablespoons tomato sauce

2 slices turkey bacon

¼ cup chopped green bell pepper (optional)

¼ cup chopped onion (optional)

1¼ cups egg substitute

¼ teaspoon black pepper

½ cup (2 ounces) shredded Cheddar cheese

1. Separate biscuits. Make indentation in center of each biscuit. Spoon 1 tablespoon tomato sauce into center.

2. Cook bacon, bell pepper and onion, if desired, in large nonstick skillet over medium-high heat until crisp. Remove bacon to paper towels. Drain drippings from skillet.

3. Spray same skillet with nonstick cooking spray. Add egg substitute; season with black pepper. Cook about 1 minute, stirring often, until eggs are set.

4. Spoon eggs evenly into biscuit centers. Crumble bacon; sprinkle over eggs. Top with cheese.

5. Preheat air fryer to 370°F. Cook in batches 6 to 8 minutes or until pizza edges are golden brown.

Variation: Try substituting low-fat sausage for the bacon in this recipe. Or, try another of your favorite cheeses in place of the Cheddar.

Breakfast Pepperoni Flatbread
MAKES 2 SERVINGS

1 flatbread

½ cup (2 ounces) shredded mozzarella cheese

1 plum tomato, diced

12 slices turkey pepperoni, cut into quarters

1 teaspoon grated Parmesan cheese

¼ cup chopped fresh basil

1. Preheat air fryer to 370°F. Place flatbread on parchment paper. Sprinkle with mozzarella cheese, tomatoes, pepperoni and Parmesan cheese.

2. Cook 3 to 5 minutes or until cheese is melted. Sprinkle with basil. Cool slightly before cutting.

Breakfast Empanadas

MAKES 4 SERVINGS

1 package (15 ounces) refrigerated pie crusts (2 crusts)

9 eggs, divided

1 teaspoon water

1 teaspoon salt

Dash black pepper

1 tablespoon butter

½ pound bacon (about 10 slices), crisp-cooked and cut into ¼-inch pieces

2 cups (8 ounces) Mexican-style shredded cheese, divided

4 tablespoons salsa

1. Place pie crusts on flat surface; cut into halves to make four semicircles.

2. Beat 1 egg and water in small bowl until well blended; set aside. Beat remaining 8 eggs, salt and pepper in medium bowl until well blended. Heat large skillet over medium heat. Add butter; tilt skillet to coat bottom. Sprinkle bacon evenly in skillet. Pour eggs into skillet; cook 2 minutes without stirring. Gently start stirring until eggs form large curds and are still slightly moist. Transfer to plate to cool.

3. Spoon one fourth of cooled scrambled egg mixture onto half of each pie crust. Reserve ¼ cup cheese; sprinkle remaining cheese evenly over eggs. Top with salsa.

4. Brush inside edges of each semicircle with reserved egg-water mixture. Fold dough over top of egg mixture and seal edges with fork. (Flour fork tines to prevent sticking, if necessary.) Brush tops of empanadas with remaining egg-water mixture; sprinkle with reserved ¼ cup cheese.

5. Preheat air fryer to 370°F. Spray basket with nonstick cooking spray.

6. Cook in batches 10 to 12 minutes or until golden.

Tip: These make a great main dish for dinner, too. Plus, they can be prepared early in the day and reheated in a preheated 350°F oven for 20 to 25 minutes.

French Toast Sticks

MAKES 4 SERVINGS

4 eggs
⅓ cup reduced-fat (2%) milk
1 teaspoon ground cinnamon
1 teaspoon vanilla

4 slices Italian bread, cut into
   3 portions each
1 teaspoon powdered sugar
¼ cup maple syrup

1. Combine eggs, milk, cinnamon and vanilla in large shallow dish.

2. Dip bread sticks in egg mixture to coat.

3. Preheat air fryer to 370°F. Line basket with parchment paper; spray with nonstick cooking spray.

4. Cook in batches 8 to 10 minutes or until golden brown. Dust lightly with powdered sugar; serve with maple syrup.

Air-Fried Parmesan Pickle Chips

MAKES 4 SERVINGS

- 4 large whole dill pickles
- ½ cup all-purpose flour
- ½ teaspoon salt
- 2 eggs
- ½ cup panko bread crumbs
- 2 tablespoons grated Parmesan cheese
- ½ cup garlic aioli mayonnaise or ranch dressing

1. Line baking sheet with paper towels. Slice pickles diagonally into ¼-inch slices, place on prepared baking sheet. Pat dry on top with paper towels to remove any moisture from pickles.

2. Combine flour and salt in shallow dish. Beat eggs in another shallow dish. Combine panko and Parmesan cheese in third shallow dish.

3. Coat pickles in flour. Dip in egg, letting excess drip back into dish, then coat in panko.

4. Preheat air fryer to 390°F. Cook in batches 8 to 10 minutes or until golden brown. Remove carefully. Serve with aioli or dressing.

Easy Wonton Chips

MAKES 2 DOZEN CHIPS

1½	teaspoons soy sauce	½	teaspoon sugar
1	teaspoon peanut or vegetable oil	¼	teaspoon garlic salt
		12	wonton wrappers

1. Combine soy sauce, oil, sugar and garlic salt in small bowl; mix well.

2. Cut wonton wrappers diagonally in half. Spray with nonstick cooking spray. Brush soy sauce mixture lightly over both sides.

3. Preheat air fryer to 370°F. Cook in batches 3 to 5 minutes, shaking halfway through cooking, until crisp and lightly browned. Transfer to wire rack; cool completely.

Pesto-Parmesan Twists

MAKES 24 BREADSTICKS

1 package (11 ounces)
   refrigerated bread dough
  All-purpose flour, for dusting
¼ cup prepared pesto

⅔ cup grated Parmesan cheese,
   divided
1 tablespoon olive oil

1. Roll out dough into 20×10-inch rectangle on lightly floured surface. Spread pesto evenly over half of dough; sprinkle with ⅓ cup Parmesan cheese. Fold remaining half of dough over filling, forming 10-inch square.

2. Cut into 12 (1-inch) strips with sharp knife. Cut strips in half crosswise to form 24 strips total. Twist each strip several times.

3. Brush breadsticks with oil; sprinkle with remaining ⅓ cup Parmesan cheese.

4. Preheat air fryer to 370°F. Cook in batches 8 to 10 minutes or until golden brown. Serve warm.

Roasted Chickpeas

MAKES 1 CUP

---

1 can (about 15 ounces) chickpeas, rinsed and drained

2 tablespoons olive oil

½ teaspoon salt

½ teaspoon black pepper

½ tablespoon chili powder

¼ teaspoon ground red pepper

1 lime, cut into wedges (optional)

---

1. Combine chickpeas, oil, salt and black pepper in large bowl; toss to mix.

2. Preheat air fryer to 390°F.

3. Cook 8 to 10 minutes, shaking occasionally during cooking, until chickpeas begin to brown.

4. Sprinkle with chili powder and ground red pepper. Serve with lime wedges, if desired.

Happy Apple Salsa with Cinnamon Pita Chips

MAKES 3 SERVINGS

2 teaspoons sugar

¼ teaspoon ground cinnamon

2 pita bread rounds, split

1 tablespoon jelly or jam

1 medium apple, diced

1 tablespoon finely diced celery

1 tablespoon finely diced carrot

1 tablespoon golden raisins

1 teaspoon lemon juice

1. Combine sugar and cinnamon in small bowl. Cut pita rounds into wedges. Spray with nonstick cooking spray; sprinkle with cinnamon-sugar.

2. Preheat air fryer to 330°F.

3. Cook 8 to 10 minutes, shaking occasionally, until lightly browned. Set aside to cool.

4. Meanwhile, place jelly in medium microwavable bowl; microwave on HIGH 10 seconds. Stir in apple, celery, carrot, raisins and lemon juice. Serve salsa with pita chips.

Herbed Potato Chips

MAKES 2 SERVINGS

1 tablespoon minced fresh dill, thyme or rosemary leaves *or* 1 teaspoon dried dill weed, thyme or rosemary

¼ teaspoon garlic salt

⅛ teaspoon black pepper

2 medium red potatoes

¾ cup sour cream

1. Combine dill, garlic salt and pepper in small bowl; set aside.

2. Cut potatoes crosswise into very thin slices, about $\frac{1}{16}$ inch thick. Pat dry with paper towels. Spray potatoes with nonstick cooking spray; sprinkle with seasoning mixture.

3. Preheat air fryer to 390°F. Line basket with parchment paper; spray with cooking spray.

4. Cook 10 to 12 minutes, shaking and spraying with cooking spray occasionally during cooking.

5. Cool. Serve with sour cream.

Kale Chips

MAKES 6 SERVINGS

1 large bunch kale (about 1 pound)

1 tablespoon olive oil

1 teaspoon garlic powder

½ teaspoon salt

½ teaspoon black pepper

1. Wash kale and pat dry with paper towels. Remove center ribs and stems; discard. Cut leaves into 2- to 3-inch-wide pieces.

2. Combine leaves, oil, garlic powder, salt and pepper in large bowl; toss to coat.

3. Preheat air fryer to 390°F.

4. Cook in batches 3 to 4 minutes or until edges are lightly browned and leaves are crisp. Cool completely. Store in airtight container.

Savory Pita Chips

MAKES 4 SERVINGS

2 whole wheat or white pita bread rounds	1 teaspoon dried basil
3 tablespoons grated Parmesan cheese	¼ teaspoon garlic powder

1. Carefully cut each pita round in half horizontally; split into two rounds. Cut each round into six wedges. Spray wedges with nonstick cooking spray.

2. Combine Parmesan cheese, basil and garlic powder in small bowl; sprinkle evenly over pita wedges.

3. Preheat air fryer to 350°F.

4. Cook 8 to 10 minutes, shaking occasionally during cooking, until golden brown. Cool completely.

Cinnamon Crisps: Substitute butter-flavored cooking spray for olive oil cooking spray and 1 tablespoon sugar mixed with ¼ teaspoon ground cinnamon for Parmesan cheese, basil and garlic powder.

Speedy Salami Spirals

MAKES ABOUT 28 SPIRALS

1 package (about 14 ounces) refrigerated pizza dough

1 cup (4 ounces) shredded Italian cheese blend

3 to 4 ounces thinly sliced Genoa salami

1. Unroll dough on cutting board or clean work surface; press into 15×10-inch rectangle. Sprinkle evenly with cheese; top with salami.

2. Starting with long side, tightly roll up dough and filling jelly-roll style, pinching seam to seal. Cut roll crosswise into ½-inch slices. (If roll is too soft to cut, refrigerate or freeze until firm.)

3. Preheat air fryer to 390°F. Line basket with parchment paper.

4. Cook in batches 8 to 10 minutes or until golden brown. Serve warm.

Spicy Baked Sweet Potato Chips

MAKES 4 SERVINGS

1 teaspoon sugar

½ teaspoon smoked paprika

¼ teaspoon salt

¼ teaspoon ground red pepper

2 medium sweet potatoes, unpeeled and cut into very thin slices

2 teaspoons vegetable oil

1. Combine sugar, paprika, salt and ground red pepper in small bowl; set aside.

2. Place potatoes in large bowl; drizzle with oil; toss to coat. Sprinkle with seasoning mixture.

3. Preheat air fryer to 390°F. Cook in batches 12 to 15 minutes, shaking occasionally, until chips are lightly browned and crisp. Cool completely.

Cinnamon Toast Poppers

MAKES 12 SERVINGS

6 cups fresh bread* cubes
(1-inch cubes)

2 tablespoons butter, melted

1 tablespoon plus 1½ teaspoons
sugar

½ teaspoon ground cinnamon

*Use a firm sourdough, whole wheat
or semolina bread.

1. Place bread cubes in large bowl. Drizzle with butter; toss to coat.

2. Combine sugar and cinnamon in small bowl. Sprinkle over bread cubes; mix well.

3. Preheat air fryer to 350°F. Cook 10 to 12 minutes, shaking occasionally during cooking, until bread is golden and fragrant. Serve warm or at room temperature.

Porky Pinwheels

MAKES 24 PINWHEELS

1 sheet puff pastry (half of 17¼-ounce package), thawed

1 egg white, beaten

8 slices bacon, crisp-cooked and crumbled

2 tablespoons packed brown sugar

¼ teaspoon ground red pepper

1. Place pastry on sheet of parchment paper. Brush with egg white.

2. Combine bacon, brown sugar and ground red pepper in small bowl. Sprinkle evenly over top of pastry; press lightly to adhere. Roll pastry jelly-roll style from long end. Wrap in parchment paper. Refrigerate 30 minutes.

3. Preheat air fryer to 370°F. Line basket with parchment paper. Slice pastry into ½-inch-thick slices.

4. Cook in batches 8 to 10 minutes or until light golden brown. Remove to wire racks; cool completely.

Bite-You-Back Roasted Edamame

MAKES 4 SERVINGS

2 teaspoons vegetable oil

2 teaspoons honey

¼ teaspoon wasabi powder*

1 package (about 12 ounces) shelled edamame, thawed if frozen

Kosher salt (optional)

Wasabi powder can be found in the Asian section of most supermarkets and in Asian specialty markets.

1. Combine oil, honey and wasabi powder in large bowl; mix well. Add edamame; toss to coat.

2. Preheat air fryer to 370°F.

3. Cook 12 to 14 minutes, shaking occasionally during cooking, until lightly browned. Remove from basket to large bowl; sprinkle generously with salt, if desired. Cool completely before serving. Store in airtight container.

Beet Chips

MAKES 2 TO 3 SERVINGS

3 medium beets (red and/or golden), trimmed

1½ tablespoons extra virgin olive oil

¼ teaspoon salt

¼ teaspoon black pepper

1. Cut beets into very thin slices, about ⅛ inch thick. Combine beets, oil, salt and pepper in medium bowl; gently toss to coat.

2. Preheat air fryer to 390°F.

3. Cook 15 to 18 minutes or until darkened and crisp. Cool completely.

Super Salami Twists

MAKES 12 SERVINGS

1 egg

1 tablespoon milk

1 cup (about ¼ pound) finely chopped hard salami

2 tablespoons yellow cornmeal

1 teaspoon Italian seasoning

1 package (about 11 ounces) refrigerated breadstick dough (12 breadsticks)

¾ cup pasta sauce, heated

1. Beat egg and milk in shallow dish until well blended. Combine salami, cornmeal and Italian seasoning in separate shallow dish.

2. Unroll breadstick dough. Separate into 12 pieces along perforations. Roll each piece of dough in egg mixture, then in salami mixture, gently pressing salami into dough. Twist each piece of dough twice.

3. Preheat air fryer to 370°F. Line basket with parchment paper.

4. Cook in batches 8 to 10 minutes or until golden brown. Remove to wire rack; cool 5 minutes. Serve warm with pasta sauce for dipping.

Corn Tortilla Chips

MAKES 6 DOZEN CHIPS

---

6 (6-inch) corn tortillas,
   preferably day-old

½ teaspoon salt
   Prepared guacamole or salsa

---

1. If tortillas are fresh, let stand, uncovered, in single layer on wire rack 1 to 2 hours to dry slightly.

2. Stack tortillas; cut tortillas into 6 or 8 equal wedges. Spray tortillas generously with nonstick olive oil cooking spray.

3. Preheat air fryer to 370°F.

4. Cook in batches 5 to 6 minutes, shaking halfway through cooking. Sprinkle with salt. Serve with guacamole or salsa, if desired.

Note: Tortilla chips are served with salsa as a snack, used as the base for nachos and used as scoops for guacamole, other dips or refried beans. They are best eaten fresh, but can be stored, tightly covered, in a cool place 2 or 3 days.

Cinnamon-Sugar Twists

MAKES 14 TWISTS

---

1 package (8 ounces) refrigerated crescent roll dough

½ cup coarse sugar

1 teaspoon ground cinnamon

---

1. Unroll dough on work surface. Cut crosswise into 1-inch strips. Roll strips to form thin ropes; fold in half and twist halves together. Combine sugar and cinnamon in shallow dish.

2. Preheat air fryer to 370°F. Line basket with parchment paper; spray with nonstick cooking spray.

3. Cook in batches 6 to 8 minutes or until golden brown. Spray with cooking spray; roll in cinnamon-sugar mixture to coat. Serve warm.

Thick Potato Chips with Beer Ketchup

MAKES 4 SERVINGS

Beer Ketchup (recipe follows)

2 baking potatoes

Sea salt and black pepper

1. Prepare Beer Ketchup; set aside. Preheat air fryer to 390°F.

2. Slice potatoes into ⅛- to ¼-inch-thick slices; place in large bowl. Spray with nonstick cooking spray. Sprinkle with salt and pepper.

3. Cook in batches 12 to 15 minutes, shaking occasionally during cooking, until crispy and golden brown.

4. Serve with Beer Ketchup.

Beer Ketchup

MAKES ABOUT 1 CUP

¾ cup ketchup

¼ cup beer

1 tablespoon Worcestershire sauce

¼ teaspoon onion powder

Ground red pepper

Mix all ingredients in small saucepan. Bring to a boil. Reduce heat; simmer 2 to 3 minutes. Remove from heat and let cool. Cover and store in refrigerator until ready to use.

Spiced Sesame Wonton Crisps

MAKES 4 SERVINGS

1 tablespoon water

2 teaspoons olive oil

½ teaspoon paprika

½ teaspoon ground cumin or chili powder

¼ teaspoon dry mustard

10 (3-inch) wonton wrappers, cut in strips

Sesame seeds

1. Combine water, oil, paprika, cumin and mustard in small bowl; mix well.

2. Lightly brush wonton strips with oil mixture. Sprinkle with sesame seeds.

3. Preheat air fryer to 350°F. Spray basket with nonstick cooking spray.

4. Cook in single layer in batches 4 to 5 minutes or until browned and crunchy, shaking halfway through cooking. Remove to plate; cool completely.

Note: Your wonton crisps may curl up in the air fryer while cooking.

Everything Seasoning Dip with Bagel Chips

MAKES ABOUT 2 CUPS DIP

2 large bagels, sliced vertically into rounds

Butter-flavored nonstick cooking spray

1 container (12 ounces) whipped cream cheese

1½ tablespoons green onion tops, chopped

1 teaspoon minced onion

1 teaspoon minced garlic

1 teaspoon sesame seeds

1 teaspoon poppy seeds

¼ teaspoon kosher salt

1. Preheat air fryer to 360°F.

2. Coat bagel rounds generously with cooking spray. Cook 7 to 8 minutes until golden brown, shaking occasionally.

3. Combine cream cheese, green onion, minced onion, garlic, sesame seeds, poppy seeds and salt in medium bowl; stir to blend.

4. Serve chips with dip.

Grilled Pesto, Ramen and Cheese Sandwich

MAKES 4 SERVINGS

1 package (3 ounces) ramen noodles, any flavor*	8 slices French or Italian bread
¼ cup prepared pesto	4 slices provolone cheese
3 tablespoons butter	1 tomato, cut into slices
	Discard seasoning packet.

1. Prepare noodles according to package directions; rinse and drain well. Place noodles in medium bowl; add pesto, stirring to mix well.

2. Spread butter on one side of each slice bread. Divide noodle mixture among four slices bread, butter-side out. Top each with 1 slice cheese, 1 slice tomato and remaining bread slices.

3. Preheat air fryer to 370°F. Cook in batches 3 to 5 minutes or until sandwiches are golden brown and cheese is melted.

Pizza-Stuffed Potatoes

MAKES 2 SERVINGS

2 medium baking potatoes

¾ cup pizza sauce

⅛ teaspoon garlic powder

2 teaspoons grated Parmesan cheese

1 ounce turkey pepperoni slices (about 16), quartered

¾ cup shredded part-skim mozzarella cheese

1. Poke potatoes with fork and cook in microwave on HIGH 5 to 7 minutes* or until soft. Split potatoes open with a knife; mash insides lightly.

2. Top each potato with 3 tablespoons pizza sauce. Sprinkle potatoes evenly with garlic powder and Parmesan cheese. Top evenly with pepperoni and mozzarella cheese.

3. Preheat air fryer to 370°F. Line basket with parchment paper.

4. Cook 4 to 6 minutes or until cheese is melted.

You can also cook the potatoes in your air fryer. Preheat air fryer to 390°F. Cook potatoes 35 to 40 minutes, turning halfway during cooking.

Baked Pork Buns

MAKES 10 SERVINGS

1 tablespoon oil

2 cups coarsely chopped bok choy

1 small onion or large shallot, thinly sliced

1 container (18 ounces) refrigerated shredded barbecue pork

All-purpose flour, for dusting

2 packages (10 ounces each) refrigerated jumbo buttermilk biscuit dough (5 biscuits per package)

1. Heat oil in large skillet over medium-high heat. Add bok choy and onion; cook and stir 8 to 10 minutes or until vegetables are tender. Remove from heat; stir in barbecue pork.

2. Lightly flour work surface. Separate biscuits; split each biscuit in half to create two thin biscuits. Flatten each biscuit half into 5-inch circle.

3. Spoon heaping tablespoon of pork mixture onto one side of each circle. Fold dough over filling to form half circle; press edges to seal.

4. Preheat air fryer to 350°F. Line basket with parchment paper; spray with nonstick cooking spray.

5. Cook in batches 8 to 10 minutes or until golden brown.

Pizza Sandwich

MAKES 4 TO 6 SERVINGS

1 loaf (12 ounces) focaccia
½ cup pizza sauce
20 slices pepperoni
8 slices (1 ounce each)
   mozzarella cheese

1 can (2¼ ounces) sliced
   mushrooms, drained
   Red pepper flakes (optional)
   Olive oil

1. Cut focaccia horizontally in half. Spread cut sides of both halves with pizza sauce. Layer bottom half with pepperoni, cheese and mushrooms; sprinkle with red pepper flakes, if desired. Cover with top half of focaccia. Brush sandwich lightly with oil.*

2. Preheat air fryer to 370°F.

3. Cook 3 to 5 minutes or until cheese melts and bread is golden brown. Cut into wedges to serve.

Depending on the size of your air fryer, you may need to cut the focaccia vertically in half to fit.

Note: Focaccia can be found in the bakery section of most supermarkets. It is often available in different flavors, such as tomato, herb, cheese or onion.

Buffalo Chicken Wraps

MAKES 2 SERVINGS

2 boneless skinless chicken breasts (about 4 ounces each)

4 tablespoons buffalo wing sauce, divided

1 cup broccoli slaw

1½ teaspoons light blue cheese salad dressing

2 (8-inch) whole wheat tortillas, warmed

1. Place chicken in large resealable food storage bag. Add 2 tablespoons buffalo sauce; seal bag. Marinate in refrigerator 15 minutes.

2. Meanwhile, preheat air fryer to 370°F. Cook 8 to 10 minutes per side or until no longer pink. When cool enough to handle, slice chicken; combine with remaining 2 tablespoons buffalo sauce in medium bowl.

3. Combine broccoli slaw and blue cheese dressing in medium bowl; mix well.

4. Arrange chicken and broccoli slaw evenly down center of each tortilla. Roll up to secure filling. To serve, cut in half diagonally.

Tip: If you don't like the spicy flavor of buffalo wing sauce, substitute your favorite barbecue sauce.

Classic Grilled Cheese

MAKES 2 SANDWICHES

4 slices (about ¾ ounce each)
   American cheese

4 slices white bread

Butter, melted

1. Place two slices of cheese each on two bread slices; top with remaining bread slices. Brush outsides of sandwiches with butter.

2. Preheat air fryer to 350°F. Cook in batches 3 to 5 minutes per side or until cheese melts and sandwiches are golden brown.

Chicken Corndog Bites

MAKES 16 BITES

1 package (8 ounces)
   refrigerated dough sheet

1 package (9 ounces) Italian-
   seasoned cooked chicken
   breast strips

Mustard

Ketchup

1. Unroll dough on lightly floured surface. Roll into 12×9-inch rectangle; cut into 16 (4×3-inch) pieces.

2. Cut chicken strips in half crosswise. Place one piece of chicken on each piece of dough; wrap dough around chicken and seal, pressing edges together tightly.

3. Preheat air fryer to 370°F. Line basket with parchment paper or foil.

4. Cook in batches 5 to 7 minutes or until light golden brown. Decorate with mustard and ketchup. Serve warm with additional mustard and ketchup.

Southwestern Chili Cheese Empanadas
MAKES 6 TO 8 SERVINGS

¾ cup (3 ounces) finely shredded taco-flavored cheese*

⅓ cup diced green chiles, drained

1 package (15 ounces) refrigerated pie crusts (2 crusts)

1 egg

1 tablespoon water

Chili powder

If taco-flavored cheese is unavailable, toss ¾ cup shredded Colby Jack cheese with ½ teaspoon chili powder.

1. Combine cheese and chiles in small bowl.

2. Unfold one pastry crust on floured surface. Roll into 13-inch circle. Cut dough rounds using 3-inch cookie cutter, rerolling scraps as necessary. Repeat with remaining crust.

3. Spoon 1 teaspoon cheese mixture in center of each dough round. Fold round in half, sealing edge with tines of fork.

4. Place empanadas on waxed paper-lined baking sheets; freeze, uncovered, 1 hour or until firm. Place in resealable food storage bags. Freeze up to 2 months, if desired.

5. To complete recipe, preheat air fryer to 370°F. Beat egg and water in small bowl; brush on empanadas. Sprinkle with chili powder.

6. Cook in batches 8 to 10 minutes or until golden brown. Remove to wire rack to cool.

Serving Suggestion: Serve empanadas with salsa and sour cream.

Veggie Pizza Pitas
MAKES 2 SERVINGS

1 whole wheat pita bread round, cut in half horizontally (to make 2 rounds)

2 tablespoons pizza sauce

½ teaspoon dried basil

⅛ teaspoon red pepper flakes (optional)

½ cup sliced mushrooms

¼ cup thinly sliced green bell pepper

¼ cup thinly sliced red onion

½ cup (4 ounces) shredded mozzarella cheese

1 teaspoon grated Parmesan cheese

1. Arrange pita rounds, rough sides up, in single layer on parchment paper. Spread 1 tablespoon pizza sauce evenly over each round to within ¼ inch of edge. Sprinkle with basil and red pepper flakes, if desired. Top with mushrooms, bell pepper and onion. Sprinkle with mozzarella cheese.

2. Preheat air fryer to 370°F.

3. Cook 5 to 7 minutes until mozzarella cheese melts. Sprinkle ½ teaspoon Parmesan cheese over each pita round.

Note: These pitas can be served as appetizers, as well.

Sandwich Monsters

MAKES 7 SERVINGS

1 package (about 16 ounces) refrigerated jumbo buttermilk biscuit dough (8 biscuits)

1 cup (4 ounces) shredded mozzarella cheese

⅓ cup sliced mushrooms

2 ounces pepperoni slices (about 35 slices), quartered

½ cup pizza sauce, plus additional for dipping

1 egg, beaten

1. Separate biscuits; set aside one biscuit for decorations. Roll out remaining biscuits into 7-inch circles on lightly floured surface.

2. Top half of each circle evenly with cheese, mushrooms, pepperoni and sauce, leaving ½-inch border. Fold dough over filling to form semicircle; seal edges with fork. Brush tops with egg.

3. Split remaining biscuit horizontally; cut each half into eight ¼-inch strips. For each sandwich, roll two strips of dough into spirals to create eyes. Divide remaining two strips of dough into seven pieces to create noses. Arrange eyes and noses on tops of sandwiches; brush with egg.

4. Preheat air fryer to 370°F. Line basket with parchment paper or foil.

5. Cook in batches 6 to 8 minutes or until golden brown. Remove to wire rack; cool 5 minutes. Serve with additional pizza sauce.

Tip: Don't worry about leaking sauce or cheese—it will look like it's coming from the monster's mouth!

Punched Pizza Rounds

MAKES 20 SERVINGS

1 package (12 ounces) refrigerated flaky buttermilk biscuits (10 biscuits)

80 mini pepperoni slices or 20 small pepperoni slices

¼ cup chopped bell pepper (optional)

1 tablespoon dried basil

½ cup pizza sauce

1½ cups (6 ounces) shredded mozzarella cheese

Shredded Parmesan cheese (optional)

1. Spray (2½-inch) silicone muffin cups with nonstick cooking spray.

2. Separate biscuits; split each biscuit in half horizontally to create 20 rounds. Place in prepared muffin cups. Press four mini pepperoni slices into center of each round. Sprinkle with bell pepper, if desired, and basil. Spread pizza sauce over pepperoni; sprinkle with mozzarella.

3. Preheat air fryer to 370°F. Cook in batches 14 to 16 minutes or until pizzas are golden brown. Sprinkle with Parmesan cheese, if desired. Cool 2 minutes; remove to wire racks. Serve warm.

Tuna Melts

MAKES 2 SERVINGS

1   can (about 5 ounces) chunk white tuna packed in water, drained and flaked

½   cup packaged coleslaw mix

1   tablespoon sliced green onion

1   tablespoon mayonnaise

½   tablespoon Dijon mustard

¼   teaspoon dried dill weed (optional)

2   English muffins, split

¼   cup (1 ounce) shredded Cheddar cheese

1. Combine tuna, coleslaw mix and green onion in medium bowl. Combine mayonnaise, mustard and dill weed, if desired, in small bowl. Stir mayonnaise mixture into tuna mixture. Spread tuna mixture onto muffin halves.

2. Preheat air fryer to 370°F. Cook 3 to 4 minutes or until heated through and lightly browned. Sprinkle with cheese. Cook 1 to 2 minutes until cheese melts.

Chicken Salad with Creamy Tarragon Dressing

MAKES 4 SERVINGS

Creamy Tarragon Dressing
(recipe follows)

1 pound chicken tenders

1 teaspoon Cajun or Creole
seasoning*

1 package (10 ounces) mixed
salad greens

2 unpeeled apples, cored and
thinly sliced

1 cup packed alfalfa sprouts

2 tablespoons raisins

*Adjust your seasoning if you prefer
more or less of a spicier taste.*

1. Prepare Creamy Tarragon Dressing. Preheat air fryer to 370°F.

2. Season chicken with Cajun seasoning. Spray chicken with nonstick cooking spray. Cook in batches 10 to 12 minutes or until no longer pink in center.

3. Divide salad greens among four large plates. Arrange chicken, apples and sprouts on top of greens. Sprinkle with raisins. Serve with dressing.

Creamy Tarragon Dressing

MAKES ABOUT 1 CUP

½ cup plain yogurt

¼ cup sour cream

¼ cup frozen apple juice
concentrate

1 tablespoon spicy brown
mustard

1 tablespoon minced fresh
tarragon leaves

Combine all ingredients in small bowl.

Vegetable and Hummus Muffaletta

MAKES 6 SERVINGS

1 small eggplant, cut lengthwise into ⅛-inch slices

1 yellow squash, cut lengthwise into ⅛-inch slices

1 zucchini, cut on the diagonal into ⅛-inch slices

1 tablespoon extra virgin olive oil

½ teaspoon salt

¼ teaspoon black pepper

1 boule or round bread (8 inches), cut in half horizontally

1 container (8 ounces) hummus, any flavor

1 jar (12 ounces) roasted red bell peppers, drained

1 jar (6 ounces) marinated artichoke hearts, drained and chopped

1 small tomato, thinly sliced

1. Combine eggplant, squash, zucchini, oil, salt and black pepper in large bowl; toss to coat.

2. Preheat air fryer to 390°F. Cook vegetables in batches 4 to 6 minutes, shaking halfway during cooking, until tender and golden. Cool to room temperature.

3. Scoop out bread from both halves of boule, leaving about 1 inch of bread on edges and about 1½ inches on bottom. (Reserve bread for bread crumbs or croutons.) Spread hummus evenly on inside bottom of bread. Layer vegetables, roasted peppers, artichokes and tomato over hummus; cover with top half of bread. Wrap stuffed loaf tightly in plastic wrap. Refrigerate at least 1 hour before cutting into wedges.

Substitution: You can substitute red bell peppers for the jarred peppers and roast in the air fryer. Preheat air fryer to 390°F. Cook 15 minutes, turning once or twice. Let sit in air fryer 10 minutes longer to loosen skin. Carefully remove skin with paring knife.

Bell Pepper and Ricotta Calzones

MAKES 6 SERVINGS

2 teaspoons olive oil

1 medium red bell pepper, diced

1 medium green bell pepper, diced

1 small onion, diced

½ teaspoon Italian seasoning

⅛ teaspoon black pepper

1 clove garlic, minced

1¼ cups marinara sauce, divided

¼ cup ricotta cheese

⅛ cup mozzarella cheese

1 package (14 ounces) refrigerated pizza dough

1. Heat oil in medium nonstick skillet over medium heat. Add bell peppers, onion, Italian seasoning and black pepper. Cook about 8 minutes, stirring occasionally until vegetables are tender. Add garlic, and cook, stirring constantly, 1 minute. Stir in ½ cup marinara sauce; cook about 2 minutes until thickened slightly. Transfer vegetable mixture to plate; let cool slightly.

2. Combine ricotta cheese and mozzarella cheese in small bowl. Unroll dough and cut into six 4×4-inch squares. Pat each square into 5×5-inch square. Spoon ⅓ cup vegetable mixture into center of each square. Top vegetables with 1 tablespoon cheese mixture. Fold dough over filling to form triangle; pinch and fold edges together to seal.

3. Preheat air fryer to 370°F. Line basket with parchment paper.

4. Cook in batches 8 to 10 minutes or until lightly browned. Cool 5 minutes. Serve with remaining marinara sauce.

Teriyaki Salmon

MAKES 2 SERVINGS

¼ cup dark sesame oil

Juice of 1 lemon

¼ cup soy sauce

2 tablespoons packed brown sugar

1 clove garlic, minced

2 salmon fillets (about 4 ounces each)

Hot cooked rice

Toasted sesame seeds and green onions (optional)

1. Whisk oil, lemon juice, soy sauce, brown sugar and garlic in medium bowl. Place salmon in large resealable food storage bag; add marinade. Refrigerate at least 2 hours.

2. Preheat air fryer to 350°F. Spray basket with nonstick cooking spray.

3. Cook 8 to 10 minutes until salmon is crispy and easily flakes when tested with a fork. Serve with rice and garnish as desired.

Parmesan Fried Chicken

MAKES 4 SERVINGS

½ cup mayonnaise

4 boneless skinless chicken breasts

¼ cup Italian seasoned dry bread crumbs

2 tablespoons grated Parmesan cheese

1. Spread mayonnaise generously over chicken. Combine bread crumbs and Parmesan cheese in shallow dish.

2. Coat chicken with bread crumb mixture.

3. Preheat air fryer to 370°F.

4. Cook 12 to 14 minutes or until golden brown.

Chicken Air-Fried Steak with Creamy Gravy

MAKES 4 TO 6 SERVINGS

½ cup all-purpose flour
½ teaspoon kosher salt
½ teaspoon onion powder
¼ teaspoon paprika
¼ teaspoon ground red pepper
⅛ teaspoon black pepper
1 large egg
¼ cup water
1 pound cube steak, divided
   into 4 to 6 portions

Gravy

1½ tablespoons butter
2 to 3 tablespoons all-purpose
   flour
¾ cup chicken broth
½ cup milk
   Salt and black pepper

1. Combine ½ cup flour, kosher salt, onion powder, paprika, ground red pepper and black pepper in shallow dish. Whisk egg and water in another shallow dish.

2. Dredge steaks in flour mixture, then egg mixture, letting excess drain back into dish, then again in flour mixture to coat well.

3. Preheat air fryer to 370°F. Spray basket with nonstick cooking spray or line with parchment paper sprayed with cooking spray.

4. Cook in batches 12 to 14 minutes, turning halfway through cooking, until steaks are browned and no longer pink in middle. Remove to serving plate.

5. For gravy, melt butter in small skillet over medium heat. Add 2 tablespoons flour, broth and milk. Cook and stir until slightly thickened. If necessary, add additional 1 tablespoon flour to thicken. Season with salt and pepper. Serve steaks with gravy.

Fried Buttermilk Chicken Fingers

MAKES 4 SERVINGS

Chicken

- 1½ cups biscuit baking mix (regular, not low-fat)
- 1 cup buttermilk*
- 1 egg, beaten
- 12 chicken tenders (about 1½ pounds), rinsed and patted dry

Dipping Sauce

- ⅓ cup mayonnaise
- 1 tablespoon honey
- 1 tablespoon prepared mustard
- 1 tablespoon packed dark brown sugar

If you don't have buttermilk, substitute 1 tablespoon vinegar or lemon juice plus enough milk to equal 1 cup. Let stand 5 minutes.

1. Place biscuit mix in pie pan or shallow dish. Combine buttermilk and egg in another shallow dish; mix until well blended.

2. Roll chicken pieces in biscuit mix, one at a time, coating evenly on all sides. Dip each chicken piece in buttermilk mixture; roll in biscuit mix again to coat evenly.

3. Preheat air fryer to 390°F. Cook in batches 10 to 12 minutes or until golden.

4. For dipping sauce, combine mayonnaise, honey, mustard and brown sugar in small bowl. Serve with chicken.

Easy Air-Fried Chicken Thighs

MAKES 4 SERVINGS

8 bone-in or boneless chicken thighs with skin
1 teaspoon garlic powder
1 teaspoon onion powder
1 teaspoon dried oregano

1 teaspoon ground thyme
1 teaspoon paprika
1 teaspoon salt
1 teaspoon black pepper

1. Place chicken in large resealable food storage bag. Combine garlic powder, onion powder, oregano, thyme, paprika, salt and pepper in small bowl; mix well. Add to chicken; shake until spices are distributed.

2. Preheat air fryer to 350°F. Line basket with parchment paper; spray with nonstick cooking spray.

3. Cook in batches 20 to 25 minutes until golden browned and cooked throughout, turning chicken halfway through cooking.

Note: Try this chicken with other favorite spices as well.

Greek Chicken Burgers with Cucumber Yogurt Sauce

MAKES 4 SERVINGS

½ cup plus 2 tablespoons plain nonfat Greek yogurt

½ medium cucumber, peeled, seeded and finely chopped

Juice of ½ lemon

3 cloves garlic, minced, divided

2 teaspoons finely chopped fresh mint *or* ½ teaspoon dried mint

⅛ teaspoon salt

⅛ teaspoon ground white pepper

Burgers

1 pound ground chicken breast

3 ounces reduced-fat crumbled feta cheese

4 large kalamata olives, rinsed, patted dry and minced

1 egg

½ to 1 teaspoon dried oregano

¼ teaspoon black pepper

Mixed baby lettuce (optional)

Fresh mint leaves (optional)

1. Combine yogurt, cucumber, lemon juice, 2 cloves garlic, 2 teaspoons chopped mint, salt and white pepper in medium bowl; mix well. Cover and refrigerate until ready to serve.

2. For burgers, combine chicken, cheese, olives, egg, oregano, black pepper and remaining 1 clove garlic in large bowl; mix well. Shape mixture into four patties.

3. Preheat air fryer to 370°F. Spray basket with nonstick cooking spray. Cook 12 to 15 minutes or until cooked through (165°F).

4. Serve burgers with sauce and mixed greens, if desired. Garnish with mint leaves.

Buttermilk Air-Fried Chicken

MAKES 4 SERVINGS

1 cut-up whole chicken (2½ to 3 pounds)
1 cup buttermilk
¾ cup all-purpose flour

½ teaspoon salt
½ teaspoon ground red pepper
¼ teaspoon garlic powder
2 cups plain dry bread crumbs

1. Place chicken pieces in large resealable food storage bag. Pour buttermilk over chicken. Close and refrigerate; let marinate at least 2 hours.

2. Preheat air fryer to 390°F. Spray basket with nonstick cooking spray.

3. Combine flour, salt, ground red pepper and garlic powder in large shallow dish. Place bread crumbs in another shallow dish.

4. Remove chicken pieces from buttermilk; coat with flour mixture then coat in bread crumbs. Spray chicken with cooking spray. Cook 20 to 25 minutes or until brown and crisp on all sides and cooked through (165°F). Serve warm.

Baked Panko Chicken

MAKES 2 SERVINGS

½ cup panko bread crumbs	Salt and black pepper
3 teaspoons assorted dried herbs (such as rosemary, basil, parsley, thyme or oregano), divided	2 tablespoons mayonnaise
	2 boneless skinless chicken breasts

1. Combine panko, 1 teaspoon herbs, salt and pepper in shallow dish. Combine mayonnaise and remaining 2 teaspoons herbs in small bowl. Spread mayonnaise mixture onto chicken. Coat chicken with panko mixture, pressing to adhere.

2. Preheat air fryer to 390°F. Line basket with parchment paper; spray with nonstick cooking spray.

3. Cook 18 to 20 until chicken is browned and no longer pink in center.

Pecan-Crusted Chicken Salad

MAKES 4 SERVINGS

Chicken

- ½ cup all-purpose flour
- ½ cup milk
- 1 egg
- ⅔ cup corn flake crumbs
- ⅔ cup finely chopped pecans
- ¾ teaspoon salt
- 4 boneless skinless chicken breasts (1¼-1½ pounds total)

Salad

- 10 cups mixed greens (1-pound package)
- 2 cans (11 ounces each) mandarin oranges, drained
- 1 cup sliced celery
- ¾ cup dried cranberries
- ½ cup glazed pecans*
- ½ cup crumbled blue cheese
- ¾ cup prepared balsamic salad dressing or other dressing of choice

Glazed or candied pecans or walnuts are often found in the produce section of the supermarket along with other salad convenience items.

1. For chicken, place flour in shallow dish. Beat milk and egg in another shallow dish. Combine corn flake crumbs, chopped pecans and salt in third shallow dish. Dip both sides of chicken in flour, then in egg mixture, letting excess drip back into dish. Roll in crumb mixture to coat completely, pressing crumbs into chicken to adhere.

2. Preheat air fryer to 390°F. Line basket with foil or parchment paper; spray with nonstick cooking spray.

3. Cook in batches 18 to 20 minutes or until chicken is no longer pink in center. Cool completely before slicing. (Chicken can be prepared several hours in advance and refrigerated.)

4. For salad, combine mixed greens, mandarin oranges, celery, cranberries, glazed pecans and cheese in large bowl. Toss gently with ¼ cup salad dressing to coat. Divide salad among four plates. Cut chicken breasts diagonally into ½-inch slices; arrange over salads. Serve with remaining dressing.

Chicken with Herb Stuffing

MAKES 4 SERVINGS

⅓ cup fresh basil leaves

1 package (8 ounces) goat cheese with garlic and herbs

4 boneless skinless chicken breasts

1 tablespoon olive oil

---

1. Place basil in food processor; process using on/off pulsing action until chopped. Cut goat cheese into large pieces and add to food processor; process using on/off pulsing action until combined.

2. Place 1 chicken breast on cutting board and cover with plastic wrap. Pound with meat mallet until ¼ inch thick. Repeat with remaining chicken.

3. Shape about 2 tablespoons of cheese mixture into log and set in center of each chicken breast. Wrap chicken around filling to enclose completely. Tie securely with kitchen string. Drizzle with oil.

4. Preheat air fryer to 370°F. Cook 15 to 20 minutes or until chicken is cooked through and filling is hot. Allow to cool slightly, remove string and slice to serve.

Blue Cheese Stuffed Chicken Breasts

MAKES 4 SERVINGS

½ cup crumbled blue cheese	Salt and black pepper
2 tablespoons butter, softened, divided	4 bone-in skin-on chicken breasts
¾ teaspoon dried thyme	1 tablespoon lemon juice

1. Combine cheese, 1 tablespoon butter and thyme in small bowl; mix well. Season with salt and pepper.

2. Loosen chicken skin by pushing fingers between skin and meat, taking care not to tear skin. Spread cheese mixture under skin; massage skin to spread mixture evenly over chicken breast.

3. Melt remaining 1 tablespoon butter in small bowl; stir in lemon juice until blended. Brush mixture over chicken. Sprinkle with salt and pepper.

4. Preheat air fryer to 370°F. Cook 22 to 24 minutes or until chicken is cooked through.

Parmesan-Crusted Tilapia

MAKES 4 SERVINGS

⅔ cup plus 3 tablespoons grated Parmesan cheese, divided

⅔ cup panko bread crumbs

⅓ cup prepared Alfredo sauce (refrigerated or jarred)

1½ teaspoons dried parsley flakes

4 tilapia fillets (6 ounces each)

Shaved Parmesan cheese (optional)

Minced fresh parsley (optional)

1. Combine ⅔ cup grated cheese and panko in medium bowl; mix well. Combine Alfredo sauce, remaining 3 tablespoons grated cheese and parsley flakes in small bowl; mix well. Spread mixture over top of fish, coating in thick even layer. Top with panko mixture, pressing in gently to adhere.

2. Preheat air fryer to 390°F. Line basket with foil or parchment paper; spray with nonstick cooking spray.

3. Cook in batches 8 to 10 minutes or until crust is golden brown and fish begins to flake when tested with a fork. Garnish with shaved Parmesan and fresh parsley.

Spicy Salmon

MAKES 4 SERVINGS

½ teaspoon ground cumin

½ teaspoon chili powder

½ teaspoon salt

¼ teaspoon black pepper

¼ teaspoon paprika

4 salmon fillets (about 4 ounces each)

1. Combine cumin, chili powder, salt, pepper and paprika in small bowl. Rub over top of salmon.

2. Preheat air fryer to 350°F. Line basket with parchment paper; spray with nonstick cooking spray.

3. Cook 8 to 10 minutes or until salmon is lightly crispy and easily flakes when tested with a fork.

Serving Suggestion: Serve with tossed salad and rice.

Garlic Knots

MAKES 20 KNOTS

- 4 tablespoons (½ stick) butter, divided
- 1 tablespoon olive oil
- 1 tablespoon minced garlic
- ½ teaspoon salt
- ¼ teaspoon garlic powder
- 1 package (about 11 ounces) refrigerated bread dough
- ½ cup grated Parmesan cheese
- 2 tablespoons chopped fresh parsley
- ½ teaspoon dried oregano

1. Melt 2 tablespoons butter in small saucepan over low heat. Add oil, garlic, salt and garlic powder; cook over very low heat 5 minutes. Pour into small bowl; set aside.

2. Roll out dough into 8×10-inch rectangle. Cut into 20 squares. Roll each piece into 8-inch rope; tie in a knot. Brush knots with garlic mixture.

3. Preheat air fryer to 370°F. Line basket with parchment paper.

4. Cook in batches 8 to 10 minutes or until knots are lightly browned. Meanwhile, melt remaining 2 tablespoons butter. Combine Parmesan cheese, parsley and oregano in small bowl; mix well. Brush melted butter over warm knots; immediately sprinkle with cheese mixture. Cool slightly; serve warm.

Curly Air-Fried Fries

MAKES 4 SERVINGS

2 large russet potatoes, unpeeled

¼ cup finely chopped onion

1 teaspoon vegetable oil

½ teaspoon salt

¼ teaspoon black pepper

Honey mustard dipping sauce, ketchup or other favorite dipping sauce

1. Spiral potatoes with thick spiral blade of spiralizer.*

2. Place potatoes and onion in large bowl; drizzle with oil. Toss well.

3. Preheat air fryer to 390°F. Line basket with parchment paper. Cook 12 to 15 minutes or until golden brown and crispy, shaking occasionally during cooking. Sprinkle with salt and pepper.

4. Serve with dipping sauce.

*If you don't have a spiralizer, cut potatoes into thin strips.

Butternut Squash Fries

MAKES 4 SERVINGS

½ teaspoon garlic powder

¼ teaspoon salt

¼ teaspoon ground red pepper

1 butternut squash (about 2½ pounds), peeled, seeded and cut into 2-inch-thin slices

2 teaspoons vegetable oil

1. Combine garlic powder, salt and ground red pepper in small bowl; set aside.

2. Place squash in large bowl. Drizzle with oil and sprinkle with seasoning mix; gently toss to coat.

3. Preheat air fryer to 390°F. Cook in batches 16 to 18 minutes, shaking halfway during cooking, until squash is tender and begins to brown.

Green Bean Fries
MAKES 6 SERVINGS

Dipping Sauce

- ½ cup light mayonnaise
- ¼ cup light sour cream
- ¼ cup low-fat buttermilk
- ¼ cup minced peeled cucumber
- 1½ teaspoons lemon juice
- 1 clove garlic
- 1 teaspoon wasabi powder
- 1 teaspoon prepared horseradish
- ½ teaspoon dried dill weed
- ½ teaspoon dried parsley flakes
- ½ teaspoon salt

- ⅛ teaspoon ground red pepper

Green Bean Fries

- 8 ounces fresh green beans, trimmed
- ⅓ cup all-purpose flour
- ⅓ cup cornstarch
- ½ cup reduced-fat (2%) milk
- 1 egg
- ¾ cup plain dry bread crumbs
- 1 teaspoon salt
- ½ teaspoon onion powder
- ¼ teaspoon garlic powder

1. For dipping sauce, combine mayonnaise, sour cream, buttermilk, cucumber, lemon juice, garlic, wasabi powder, horseradish, dill weed, parsley flakes, salt and ground red pepper in blender; blend until smooth. Refrigerate until ready to use.

2. For green bean fries, bring large saucepan of salted water to a boil. Add green beans; cook 4 minutes or until crisp-tender. Drain and run under cold running water to stop cooking.

3. Combine flour and cornstarch in large bowl. Whisk milk and egg in another large bowl. Combine bread crumbs, salt, onion powder and garlic powder in shallow dish. Place green beans in flour mixture; toss to coat. Working in batches, coat beans with egg mixture, letting excess drain back into bowl. Roll green beans in bread crumb mixture to coat.

4. Preheat air fryer to 390°F. Cook in batches 6 to 8 minutes, shaking occasionally during cooking, until golden brown. Serve warm with dipping sauce.

Sweet Potato Fries

MAKES 2 SERVINGS

2 sweet potatoes, peeled and sliced

1 tablespoon olive oil

¼ teaspoon coarse salt

¼ teaspoon black pepper

½ cup grated Parmesan cheese (optional)

1. Toss potatoes with oil, salt and pepper in medium bowl.

2. Preheat air fryer to 390°F. Spray basket with nonstick cooking spray.

3. Cook 10 to 12 minutes, shaking occasionally during cooking, until lightly browned. Sprinkle with cheese, if desired.

Zucchini Fritte

MAKES 4 SERVINGS

Lemon Aioli (recipe follows)
¾ to 1 cup soda water
½ cup all-purpose flour
¼ cup cornstarch
½ teaspoon coarse salt, plus additional for serving
¼ teaspoon garlic powder
¼ teaspoon dried oregano
¼ teaspoon black pepper

3 cups panko bread crumbs
1½ pounds medium zucchini (about 8 inches long), ends trimmed, cut lengthwise into ¼-inch-thick slices
¼ cup grated Parmesan or Romano cheese
Chopped fresh parsley
Lemon wedges

1. Prepare Lemon Aioli; cover and refrigerate until ready to use.

2. Pour ¾ cup soda water into large bowl. Combine flour, cornstarch, ½ teaspoon salt, garlic powder, oregano and pepper in medium bowl; mix well. Gradually whisk flour mixture into soda water just until blended. Add additional soda water, if necessary, to reach consistency of thin pancake batter. Place panko in shallow dish.

3. Working with one at a time, dip zucchini slices into batter to coat; let excess batter drip back into bowl. Add to dish with panko; pressing into zucchini slices to coat both sides completely.

4. Preheat air fryer to 390°F. Line baking sheet with paper towels.

5. Cook in batches 7 to 10 minutes or until golden brown. Sprinkle with cheese and parsley. Serve with Lemon Aioli and lemon wedges.

Lemon Aioli: Combine ½ cup mayonnaise, 2 tablespoons lemon juice, 1 tablespoon chopped fresh Italian parsley and 1 clove minced garlic in small bowl; mix well. Season with salt and pepper.

Air-Fried Corn-on-the-Cob
MAKES 2 SERVINGS

2 teaspoons butter, melted

¼ teaspoon salt

½ teaspoon black pepper

½ teaspoon chopped fresh parsley

2 ears corn, husks and silks removed

Foil

Grated Parmesan cheese (optional)

1. Combine butter, salt, pepper and parsley in small bowl. Brush corn with butter mixture. Wrap each ear corn in foil.*

2. Preheat air fryer to 390°F. Cook 10 to 12 minutes, turning halfway through cooking. Sprinkle with cheese before serving, if desired.

If your air fryer basket is on the smaller side, you may need to break ears of corn in half to fit.

Oven "Fries"
MAKES 2 SERVINGS

2 small russet potatoes (10 ounces), refrigerated	¼ teaspoon salt or onion salt
2 teaspoons olive oil	

1. Peel potatoes and cut lengthwise into ¼-inch strips. Place in colander; rinse under cold running water 2 minutes. Drain. Pat dry with paper towels.

2. Preheat air fryer to 390°F. Meanwhile, place potatoes in large resealable food storage bag. Drizzle with oil. Seal bag; shake to coat evenly.

3. Cook 15 to 18 minutes, shaking occasionally during cooking, until light brown and crisp. Sprinkle with salt.

Note: Refrigerating potatoes—usually not recommended for storage— converts the starch in the potatoes to sugar, which enhances the browning when the potatoes are baked. Do not refrigerate the potatoes longer than 2 days, because they may develop a sweet flavor.

Cheesy Garlic Bread

MAKES 4 TO 6 SERVINGS

1 loaf (about 8 ounces) Italian bread	1 cup (4 ounces) shredded mozzarella cheese
¼ cup (½ stick) butter, softened	
4 cloves garlic, diced	
2 tablespoons grated Parmesan cheese	

1. Cut bread in half horizontally. Spread cut sides of bread evenly with butter; top with garlic. Sprinkle with Parmesan, then mozzarella cheeses.

2. Preheat air fryer to 370°F. Line basket with foil.

3. Cook 5 to 6 minutes or until cheeses are melted and golden brown. Cut crosswise into slices. Serve warm.

Roasted Butternut Squash

MAKES 5 SERVINGS

1 pound butternut squash, peeled and cut into 1-inch cubes (about 4 cups)

2 medium onions, coarsely chopped

8 ounces carrots, peeled and cut into ½-inch diagonal slices (about 2 cups)

1 tablespoon packed dark brown sugar

¼ teaspoon salt

Black pepper (optional)

1. Combine vegetables in large bowl. Spray with nonstick cooking spray; toss gently. Sprinkle with brown sugar, salt and pepper, if desired.

2. Preheat air fryer to 390°F. Spray basket with cooking spray.

3. Bake 20 to 25 minutes, shaking occasionally during cooking, until vegetables are tender and brown.

Parmesan-Crusted French Fries with Rosemary Dipping Sauce

MAKES 4 SERVINGS

3 medium baking potatoes (8 ounces each), peeled and cut into 12 wedges

1 tablespoon olive oil

⅛ teaspoon salt

⅛ teaspoon black pepper

¼ cup shredded Parmesan cheese

Dipping Sauce

½ cup mayonnaise

1 teaspoon chopped fresh rosemary *or* ½ teaspoon dried rosemary

½ teaspoon grated lemon peel

1 clove garlic, crushed

1. Toss potatoes with oil, salt and pepper in medium bowl.

2. Preheat air fryer to 390°F. Cook in batches 18 to 20 minutes, shaking halfway through cooking. Sprinkle Parmesan cheese over potatoes. Cook additional 3 to 5 minutes until cheese melts and potatoes are tender.

3. For Dipping Sauce, stir together mayonnaise, rosemary, lemon peel and garlic in small bowl. Serve potatoes with Dipping Sauce.

Caprese Portobellos

MAKES 4 SERVINGS

2 tablespoons butter

½ teaspoon minced garlic

1 teaspoon dried parsley flakes

4 portobello mushrooms, stems removed

1 cup (4 ounces) shredded mozzarella cheese

1 cup cherry or grape tomatoes, sliced thin

2 tablespoons fresh basil, thinly sliced

Balsamic glaze

1. Combine butter, garlic and parsley flakes in small dish. Microwave on LOW 30 seconds or until melted.

2. Wash mushrooms thoroughly; dry on paper towels. Brush both sides of mushrooms with butter mixture.

3. Preheat air fryer to 390°F. Spray basket with nonstick cooking spray.

4. Fill mushroom caps with about ¼ cup cheese each. Top with sliced tomatoes. Cook 5 to 7 minutes or until cheese is melted and lightly browned. Top with basil.

5. Drizzle with balsamic glaze before serving.

Fried Green Tomatoes

MAKES 4 SERVINGS

⅓ cup all-purpose flour

¼ teaspoon salt

2 eggs

1 tablespoon water

½ cup panko bread crumbs

2 large green tomatoes, cut into ½-inch-thick slices

½ cup ranch dressing

1 tablespoon Sriracha sauce

1 package (5 ounces) spring greens salad mix

¼ cup crumbled goat cheese

1. Combine flour and salt in shallow dish. Beat eggs and water in another shallow dish. Place panko in third shallow dish. Coat tomato slices with flour, shaking off excess. Dip in egg mixture, letting excess drip back into bowl. Roll in panko to coat. Place on plate.

2. Preheat air fryer to 390°F. Line basket with parchment paper.

3. Cook in batches 6 to 8 minutes or until golden brown.

4. Combine ranch dressing and Sriracha in small bowl; mix well. Divide greens among four serving plates; top with tomatoes. Drizzle with dressing mixture; sprinkle with cheese.

Rich Roasted Sesame Vegetables

MAKES 2 SERVINGS

1 carrot, quartered lengthwise and cut into 2-inch pieces

1 medium sweet potato, peeled and cut into ¾-inch cubes

½ red bell pepper, cut into 1-inch cubes

½ medium onion, cut into ½-inch wedges

1 tablespoon dark sesame oil

2 teaspoons sugar

¼ teaspoon salt

1. Place carrot, sweet potato, bell pepper and onion in large bowl. Sprinkle with oil, sugar and salt; toss gently to coat.

2. Preheat air fryer to 390°F. Line basket with foil.

3. Cook 10 to 12 minutes, shaking occasionally during cooking, until vegetables are tender and browned.

Tip: Before serving, sprinkle vegetables with rice vinegar or lime juice, if desired.

Cheesy Pumpkin Biscuits

MAKES 8 BISCUITS

1 package (about 16 ounces) jumbo buttermilk biscuit dough (8 biscuits)

1 tablespoon butter, melted

1 cup (4 ounces) shredded Cheddar cheese

2 green onions, finely chopped

1. Separate dough into biscuits. Lightly score tops of biscuits with paring knife to resemble lines on pumpkins. Brush with butter.

2. Preheat air fryer to 350°F. Line basket with parchment paper.

3. Cook in batches 8 to 10 minutes or until lightly browned.

4. Meanwhile, combine cheese and green onions in small bowl. Split baked biscuits horizontally into halves with fork. (Biscuits do not need to be fully separated.)

5. Spread cheese filling inside each biscuit. Return to basket. Cook in batches 1 to 2 minutes or until cheese is melted.

6. Serve warm.

Parmesan Potato Wedges

MAKES 6 SERVINGS

2 pounds unpeeled red potatoes	½ teaspoon salt
2 tablespoons butter, melted	Black pepper
1½ teaspoons dried oregano	2 tablespoons grated Parmesan cheese

1. Boil potatoes in salted water 8 to 10 minutes or until fork-tender. Drain. Cool completely.

2. Cut cooled potatoes into wedges; place in large bowl. Add butter, oregano, salt and pepper; mix gently.

3. Preheat air fryer to 390°F. Line basket with parchment paper.

4. Cook potatoes 8 to 10 minutes, shaking occasionally during cooking, until golden brown and crispy. Place in large bowl; toss with Parmesan cheese.

Fried Zucchini

MAKES 4 TO 6 SERVINGS

1 package (about 10 ounces)
  zucchini noodles

¼ cup all-purpose flour

½ teaspoon Italian seasoning

1 small egg, beaten

¾ cup panko bread crumbs

½ cup marinara sauce, heated

1. Drain any excess water from zucchini noodles; place in medium bowl. Add flour and Italian seasoning; toss until well coated. Add egg; mix until well blended.

2. Place panko in shallow dish.

3. Shape zucchini mixture into 1-inch balls. Place in panko; press panko to adhere to all sides.

4. Preheat air fryer to 390°F. Line basket with parchment paper; spray with nonstick cooking spray. Cook 8 to 10 minutes or until golden brown.

5. Serve warm with marinara sauce for dipping.

Orange Glazed Carrots

MAKES 6 SERVINGS

1 package (32 ounces) baby carrots

1 tablespoon packed light brown sugar

1 tablespoon orange juice

1 tablespoon melted butter

¼ teaspoon ground cinnamon

⅛ teaspoon ground nutmeg

Orange peel and fresh chopped parsley (optional)

1. Place carrots in large bowl. Combine brown sugar, orange juice and butter in small bowl. Pour over carrots; toss well.

2. Preheat air fryer to 390°F.

3. Cook 6 to 8 minutes, shaking occasionally during cooking, until carrots are tender and lightly browned. Remove to serving dish. Sprinkle with cinnamon and nutmeg. Garnish with orange peel and parsley, if desired.

Crispy Fries with Herbed Dipping Sauce

MAKES 3 SERVINGS

Herbed Dipping Sauce
(recipe follows)

2 large unpeeled baking
potatoes

1 tablespoon vegetable oil
½ teaspoon kosher salt

1. Prepare Herbed Dipping Sauce; set aside.

2. Cut potatoes into ¼-inch strips. Toss potato strips with oil in large bowl to coat evenly.

3. Preheat air fryer to 390°F. Spray basket with nonstick cooking spray.

4. Cook in batches 18 to 20 minutes, shaking occasionally during cooking, until golden brown and crispy. Sprinkle with salt. Serve immediately with Herbed Dipping Sauce.

Herbed Dipping Sauce: Stir ¼ cup mayonnaise, 1 tablespoon chopped fresh herbs (such as basil, parsley, oregano and/or dill), ¼ teaspoon salt and ⅛ teaspoon black pepper in small bowl until smooth and well blended. Cover and refrigerate until ready to serve.

Mixed Berry Dessert Lavash with Honeyed Mascarpone

MAKES 4 SERVINGS

1½ cups assorted mixed fresh berries

2 tablespoons honey, divided

½ teaspoon vanilla

1 piece lavash bread, 7½×9½ inches

1 tablespoon melted butter

4 ounces (½ cup) mascarpone cheese

1 tablespoon julienned fresh mint leaves

1. Place berries in medium bowl; stir in 1 tablespoon honey and vanilla. Refrigerate until ready to use.

2. Brush both sides of lavash with butter; cut into four even pieces.

3. Preheat air fryer to 370°F. Line basket with parchment paper. Cook 6 to 8 minutes, turning half way through cooking, until lavash is golden and crisp. Cool 5 minutes on wire rack.

4. Stir mascarpone and remaining 1 tablespoon honey in small bowl. Spread over each piece of lavash. Top with sweetened berries. Sprinkle with mint to serve.

Fried Pineapple with Toasted Coconut

MAKES 8 SERVINGS

1 large pineapple, cored and
cut into chunks

½ cup packed brown sugar

1 teaspoon ground cinnamon

½ teaspoon ground nutmeg

½ cup toasted coconut*

Ice cream or whipped cream
(optional)

Chopped macadamia nuts
(optional)

Maraschino cherries
(optional)

*Toast coconut in the air fryer. Place
coconut in small ramekin; cook in
preheated air fryer at 350°F for 2 to
3 minutes or until lightly browned.*

1. Place pineapple chunks in large bowl. Combine brown sugar, cinnamon
and nutmeg in small bowl; sprinkle over pineapple. Toss well. Refrigerate
30 minutes.

2. Preheat air fryer to 370°F. Spray basket with nonstick cooking spray.

3. Cook 6 to 8 minutes or until pineapple is browned and lightly crispy.
Sprinkle with coconut. Serve with ice cream or macadamia nuts, if desired
Garnish with maraschino cherries.

Bacon S'mores Bundles

MAKES 4 SERVINGS

1¼ cups mini marshmallows

¾ cup semisweet chocolate chips

¾ cup coarsely crushed graham crackers (5 whole graham crackers)

4 slices bacon, crisp-cooked and crumbled

1 package (17¼ ounces) frozen puff pastry (2 sheets), thawed

All-purpose flour, for dusting

1. Combine marshmallows, chocolate chips, graham crackers and bacon in medium bowl.

2. Unfold pastry on lightly floured surface. Roll each pastry sheet into 12-inch square; cut into four 6-inch squares. Place scant ½ cup marshmallow mixture in center of each square.

3. Brush edges of pastry squares with water. Bring edges together over filling; twist tightly to seal.

4. Preheat air fryer to 370°F. Cook in batches 6 to 8 minutes or until golden brown. Remove to wire rack; cool 5 minutes. Serve warm.

Sugar-and-Spice Twists

MAKES 12 SERVINGS

2 tablespoons granulated sugar

½ teaspoon ground cinnamon

1 package (about 11 ounces) refrigerated breadstick dough (12 breadsticks)

1. Combine sugar and cinnamon in shallow dish or plate. Separate breadsticks; roll each piece into 12-inch rope. Roll ropes in sugar-cinnamon mixture to coat. Twist each rope into pretzel shape.

2. Preheat air fryer to 370°F. Line basket with parchment paper; spray with nonstick cooking spray.

3. Cook in batches 8 to 10 minutes or until lightly browned. Remove to wire rack to cool 5 minutes. Serve warm.

Hint: Use colored sugar sprinkles in place of the granulated sugar in this recipe for a fun "twist" of color perfect for holidays, birthdays or simple everyday celebrations.

Candy Calzone
MAKES 16 SERVINGS

1 package small chocolate, peanut and nougat candy bars, chocolate peanut butter cups or other chocolate candy bar (8 bars)

1 package (about 15 ounces) refrigerated pie crusts (2 crusts)
½ cup milk chocolate chips

1. Chop candy into ¼-inch pieces.

2. Unroll pie crusts on cutting board or clean surface. Cut out 3-inch circles with biscuit cutter. Place about 1 tablespoon chopped candy on one side of each circle; fold dough over candy to form semicircle. Crimp edges with fingers or fork to seal.

3. Preheat air fryer to 370°F. Line basket with parchment paper. Cook in batches 8 to 10 minutes or until golden brown. Remove to wire rack to cool slightly.

4. Place chocolate chips in small microwavable bowl; microwave on HIGH 1 minute. Stir; microwave in 30-second intervals, stirring until smooth. Drizzle melted chocolate over calzones; serve warm.

Double-Berry Shortcakes

MAKES 8 SERVINGS

Strawberry Filling

- 2 to 3 cups fresh sliced strawberries
- 1 tablespoon sugar

Raspberry Sauce

- 1 package (10 ounces) frozen unsweetened raspberries, thawed
- 1 tablespoon sugar

Shortcakes

- 1 package (9 ounces) yellow cake mix without pudding in the mix
- 1 egg
- ½ cup cold water
- 2 teaspoons freshly grated lemon peel

Whipped Cream

- ½ cup whipping cream
- 1 tablespoon sugar

1. Combine 2 cups strawberries and 1 tablespoon sugar in medium bowl. Let stand, 30 minutes to 2 hours, stirring occasionally, until sugar dissolves.

2. Meanwhile, place raspberries in fine-wire sieve over medium bowl. Press raspberries through sieve with rubber spatula. Discard seeds and solids. Add 1 tablespoon sugar; stir until sugar is dissolved. Set aside.

3. Spray eight 2½-inch silicone muffin cups with nonstick cooking spray.

4. Combine cake mix, egg and water in large bowl; beat according to package directions. Stir in lemon peel. Spoon batter evenly into prepared muffin cups.

5. Preheat air fryer to 350°F. Cook in batches 10 to 12 minutes or until toothpick inserted into centers comes out clean. Transfer to wire rack; cool completely.

6. Beat whipping cream and 1 tablespoon sugar in chilled medium bowl with electric mixer at high speed until soft peaks form.

7. Split shortcakes in half horizontally; place bottoms on eight plates. Spoon about ¼ cup strawberries on each cake; drizzle with 1 tablespoon raspberry sauce. Top with 2 tablespoons whipped cream. Cover with shortcake tops. Dollop evenly with remaining whipped cream; drizzle with remaining raspberry sauce. Refrigerate leftovers.

Fruit Tarts

MAKES 2 SERVINGS

1 refrigerated pie crust (half of a 15-ounce package)

1 tablespoon melted butter

¼ cup apple, cherry or blueberry pie filling

Coarse sugar

1. Unroll pie crust on clean work surface; cut into four pieces. Brush butter over dough. Spread pie filling over two pieces of dough; top each with second piece of dough. Seal edges by crimping with tines of a fork. Brush tops with butter; sprinkle with sugar.

2. Preheat air fryer to 370°F. Line basket with parchment paper.

3. Cook 6 to 8 minutes or until light golden brown. Remove to plate; cool.

Chocolate Fruit Tarts

MAKES 6 TARTS

1 refrigerated pie crust (half of 15-ounce package)

All-purpose flour, for dusting

1¼ cups prepared low-fat chocolate pudding (about

4 snack-size pudding cups)

Fresh sliced strawberries, raspberries, blackberries or favorite fruit

1. Spray six 2½-inch silicone muffin cups with nonstick cooking spray. Unfold pie crust on lightly-floured surface. Let stand at room temperature 15 minutes.

2. Roll out pie crust on clean work surface; cut out six circles with 4-inch round cookie cutter. Place dough circles in muffin cups, pleating around sides of cups. (Press firmly to hold dough in place.) Prick bottom and sides with fork.

3. Preheat air fryer to 370°F. Cook in batches 8 to 10 minutes or until golden brown. Carefully remove tart shells from muffin cups. Cool completely on wire rack.

4. Fill each tart shell with about 3 tablespoons pudding; arrange fruit on top.

Maple Walnut Apple Crescent Cobbler
MAKES 8 SERVINGS

Filling

6 Golden Delicious apples (2½ pounds), peeled and thinly sliced

⅓ cup maple syrup

2 tablespoons all-purpose flour

2 teaspoons vanilla

⅛ teaspoon ground nutmeg

Topping

1 package (8 ounces) refrigerated crescent roll dough

4 teaspoons butter, melted

¼ cup chopped walnuts

2 tablespoons packed brown sugar

1. Spray eight ramekins* with nonstick cooking spray. Combine apples, syrup, flour, vanilla and nutmeg in medium bowl; toss to coat. Spoon into prepared ramekins.

2. Preheat air fryer to 370°F. Cook 12 to 14 minutes or until apples are tender but still firm.

3. Meanwhile, divide crescent roll dough into eight triangles; place on work surface. Brush top of each triangle with butter. Combine walnuts and brown sugar in small bowl; sprinkle over dough. Roll up each dough triangle to form crescent. Arrange crescents over warm apple mixture.

4. Cook 5 to 7 minutes or until filling is thick and bubbly and crescent rolls are golden brown.

*If you do not have 8 ramekins, prepare 4 at a time.

Chocolate Cherry Turnovers

MAKES 4 TURNOVERS

1 can (8 ounces) refrigerated
crescent roll dough

¾ cup semisweet chocolate
chips, divided

½ cup canned cherry pie filling

1. Unroll dough onto clean work surface; separate into four rectangles. Press perforations firmly to seal. Cut off corners of rectangles with sharp paring knife to form oval shapes.

2. Place 1 tablespoon chocolate chips on half of each oval; top with 2 tablespoons pie filling. Sprinkle with additional 1 tablespoon chocolate chips. Fold dough over filling; press edges to seal. Crimp edges with fork, if desired.

3. Preheat air fryer to 370°F. Spray basket with nonstick cooking spray.

4. Cook in batches 8 to 10 minutes or until golden brown. Cool on wire rack 5 minutes. Melt remaining chocolate chips and drizzle over turnovers. Serve warm.

Conch Shells

MAKES 24 SERVINGS

2 tablespoons butter, softened

2 tablespoons packed brown sugar

⅛ teaspoon ground cinnamon

1 can (8 ounces) refrigerated crescent roll dough

½ cup raisins

1 egg white, slightly beaten

Granulated sugar

1. Combine butter, brown sugar and cinnamon in small bowl; set aside.

2. Unroll dough and separate into pre-scored triangles. Cut each triangle into three equal size triangles. Spread one side of each triangle with about ½ teaspoon butter mixture; sprinkle evenly with raisins. Roll each triangle at a slight angle from the straight-sided base toward the triangular tip in the shape of a conch shell.

3. Brush rolls with egg white; sprinkle with granulated sugar.

4. Preheat air fryer to 370°F. Cook in batches 5 to 7 minutes or until lightly golden. Cool on wire rack.

Serving Suggestion: Design your own sea shore! Make sand by combining equal parts finely crushed graham crackers and raw sugar crystals. Spread sand on a large platter and arrange conch shells on top.

Plum-Ginger Bruschetta

MAKES 9 SERVINGS

1 sheet frozen puff pastry (half of 17¼-ounce package), thawed

2 cups chopped unpeeled firm ripe plums (about 3 medium)

2 tablespoons sugar

2 tablespoons chopped candied ginger

1 tablespoon all-purpose flour

2 teaspoons lemon juice

⅛ teaspoon ground cinnamon

2 tablespoons apple jelly *or* apricot preserves

1. Cut puff pastry sheet lengthwise into three strips. Cut each strip crosswise in thirds to make nine pieces.

2. Preheat air fryer to 370°F. Line basket with parchment paper. Cook in batches 5 to 6 minutes or until puffed and lightly browned.

3. Meanwhile, combine plums, sugar, ginger, flour, lemon juice and cinnamon in medium bowl.

4. Gently brush each puff pastry piece with about ½ teaspoon jelly; top with scant ¼ cup plum mixture. Cook in batches 1 to 2 minutes or until fruit is tender.

Doughnut Hole Fondue

MAKES 5 SERVINGS

1 can (about 6 ounces) refrigerated biscuit dough (5 biscuits)

3 tablespoons butter, divided

1 tablespoon sugar

¼ teaspoon ground cinnamon

¾ cup whipping cream

1 cup bittersweet or semisweet chocolate chips

½ teaspoon vanilla

Sliced fresh fruit, such as pineapple, strawberries and cantaloupe

1. Separate biscuits into five portions. Cut each in half; roll dough into balls to create 10 balls.

2. Place 2 tablespoons butter in small microwavable bowl. Microwave 30 seconds or until melted; stir. Combine sugar and cinnamon in small dish. Dip balls in melted butter; roll in cinnamon-sugar mixture.

3. Preheat air fryer to 370°F. Spray basket with nonstick cooking spray.

4. Cook in batches 4 to 5 minutes or until golden brown.

5. Meanwhile, heat cream in small saucepan until bubbles form around edge. Remove from heat. Add chocolate; let stand 2 minutes or until softened. Add remaining 1 tablespoon butter and vanilla; whisk until smooth. Keep warm in fondue pot or transfer to serving bowl.

6. Serve with doughnut holes and fruit.

Chocolate Rolls

MAKES 16 ROLLS

---

8 tablespoons granulated sugar, divided

1 package (15 ounces) refrigerated pie crusts (2 crusts)

1 cup semisweet chocolate chips

1 egg white

Powdered sugar (optional)

---

1. Sprinkle 2 tablespoons granulated sugar on cutting board or work surface. Roll out one pie crust over sugar. Sprinkle pie crust with 2 tablespoons granulated sugar. Using pizza wheel or sharp knife, trim away 1 inch dough from four sides to form square. (Save dough trimmings for another use or discard.)

2. Cut square in half; cut each half crosswise into four pieces to form eight small (4×2-inch) rectangles. Place heaping teaspoon chocolate chips at one short end of each rectangle; roll up, enclosing chocolate chips. Brush lightly with egg white. Repeat with remaining crust.

3. Preheat air fryer to 370°F. Spray basket with nonstick cooking spray.

4. Cook in batches 8 to 10 minutes or until lightly browned. Cool 10 minutes to serve warm, or cool completely. Sprinkle with powdered sugar, if desired.

Apple Pie Pockets

MAKES 4 SERVINGS

2 pieces lavash bread, each cut into 4 rectangles

2 tablespoons melted butter

¾ cup apple pie filling

1 egg, lightly beaten with 1 teaspoon water

½ cup powdered sugar

⅛ teaspoon ground cinnamon

2½ teaspoons milk

1. Brush one side of each piece of lavash with butter. Place half of the pieces, buttered-side down, on work surface. Spoon 3 tablespoons pie filling in center of each lavash, leaving ½-inch border uncovered. Using pastry brush, brush border with egg wash. Top with remaining lavash pieces, buttered-side up. Using tines of fork, press edges together to seal. Use paring knife to cut three small slits in center of each pie pocket.

2. Preheat air fryer to 370°F. Line basket with parchment paper.

3. Cook in batches 8 to 10 minutes or until crust is golden and crisp. Remove to wire rack; cool 15 minutes.

4. Combine powdered sugar, cinnamon and milk in small bowl; whisk until smooth. Drizzle over pockets; let stand 15 minutes to allow glaze to slightly set.

Banana Bowties

MAKES 20 BOWTIES

1 cup peeled chopped ripe
  banana (about 2 medium)

¼ cup finely chopped walnuts or
  pecans

1 tablespoon packed brown
  sugar

20 square wonton wrappers

1 egg, beaten

Chocolate syrup

1. Combine banana, nuts and brown sugar in small bowl; gently mix.

2. Arrange wonton wrappers, one at a time, on clean surface. Brush edges with egg. Place teaspoonful of banana filling in center. Fold wrapper in half, pressing edges to seal. Pinch center to form bowtie. Cover with plastic wrap and refrigerate until needed. Repeat with remaining wrappers and filling.

3. Preheat air fryer to 370°F.

4. Cook in batches 6 to 8 minutes or until golden brown. Drizzle with chocolate syrup. Serve immediately.

SIDE DISHES

SNACKS

VOLUME MEASUREMENTS (dry)

1/8 teaspoon = 0.5 mL
1/4 teaspoon = 1 mL
1/2 teaspoon = 2 mL
3/4 teaspoon = 4 mL
1 teaspoon = 5 mL
1 tablespoon = 15 mL
2 tablespoons = 30 mL
1/4 cup = 60 mL
1/3 cup = 75 mL
1/2 cup = 125 mL
2/3 cup = 150 mL
3/4 cup = 175 mL
1 cup = 250 mL
2 cups = 1 pint = 500 mL
3 cups = 750 mL
4 cups = 1 quart = 1 L

VOLUME MEASUREMENTS (fluid)

1 fluid ounce (2 tablespoons) = 30 mL
4 fluid ounces (1/2 cup) = 125 mL
8 fluid ounces (1 cup) = 250 mL
12 fluid ounces (1 1/2 cups) = 375 mL
16 fluid ounces (2 cups) = 500 mL

WEIGHTS (mass)

1/2 ounce = 15 g
1 ounce = 30 g
3 ounces = 90 g
4 ounces = 120 g
8 ounces = 225 g
10 ounces = 285 g
12 ounces = 360 g
16 ounces = 1 pound = 450 g

DIMENSIONS

1/16 inch = 2 mm
1/8 inch = 3 mm
1/4 inch = 6 mm
1/2 inch = 1.5 cm
3/4 inch = 2 cm
1 inch = 2.5 cm

OVEN TEMPERATURES

250°F = 120°C
275°F = 140°C
300°F = 150°C
325°F = 160°C
350°F = 180°C
375°F = 190°C
400°F = 200°C
425°F = 220°C
450°F = 230°C

BAKING PAN SIZES

Utensil	Size in Inches/Quarts	Metric Volume	Size in Centimeters
Baking or	8×8×2	2 L	20×20×5
Cake Pan	9×9×2	2.5 L	23×23×5
(square or	12×8×2	3 L	30×20×5
rectangular)	13×9×2	3.5 L	33×23×5
Loaf Pan	8×4×3	1.5 L	20×10×7
	9×5×3	2 L	23×13×7
Round Layer	8×1½	1.2 L	20×4
Cake Pan	9×1½	1.5 L	23×4
Pie Plate	8×1¼	750 mL	20×3
	9×1¼	1 L	23×3
Baking Dish	1 quart	1 L	—
or Casserole	1½ quart	1.5 L	—
	2 quart	2 L	—